tabletop gardens

tabletop gardens

Create 40
intimate gardens
for the home,
no matter what
the season

Rosemary McCreary

PHOTOGRAPHS BY **William Holt**

STOREY
BOOKS

*The mission of Storey Publishing is to serve our customers
by publishing practical information that encourages personal independence
in harmony with the environment.*

Edited by Gwen Steege and Karen Levy
Photo styling by Sarah Dawson
Design by Wendy Palitz with Vertigo Design
Illustrations by Brigita Fuhrmann
Indexed by Nan Badgett / word•a•bil•i•ty
Text copyright © 2002 by Rosemary McCreary
Photographs copyright © 2002 by William Holt

Printed in Italy by Sfera International
10 9 8 7 6 5 4 3 2 1

LIBRARY OF CONGRESS CATALOGING-IN-PUBLICATION DATA

McCreary, Rosemary.
Tabletop gardens : create 40 intimate, contained gardens for the home,
no matter the season / Rosemary McCreary.
p. cm.
ISBN 1-58017-466-3 (alk. paper)
1. Indoor gardening. 2. Indoor gardens. I. Title.
SB419 .M247 2002
635.9'86--dc21
2002006930

DEDICATION

To Gene, my husband, who shares my life and
love and helps me build gardens from the stuff of dreams.

ACKNOWLEDGMENTS

Special thanks to friends and the many Sonoma County
gardeners and nursery men and women who
lent support and materials, especially Carole Delorenzo
and Anita Engberg, and to Janet Sanchez,
for the confidence she inspired from the start.

Many thanks to the stores and nurseries that supplied
beautiful containers, props, and plants to create the
gardens and enhance their settings:
Berkeley Horticultural Nursery, The Gardener, and
Smith & Hawken, all of Berkeley, California; Dandelion,
Paxton Gate, and Yard Art, all of San Francisco,
California; Marquard Gardens of Santa Rosa, California;
and Bitters Co. of Seattle, Washington.

contents

creating indoor gardens

Nearly everyone has looked out upon a garden longingly and felt the pull of its vitality. Why people love gardens so much is a bit of a mystery, but nothing so enigmatic that it bears too much scrutiny. Gardens simply make us feel good. The secret of creating a beautiful miniature garden in your own home isn't terribly complicated. It's simply a matter of bringing together a harmonious combination of plants in the right site, then caring for them. Your contained garden can be an end in itself that embellishes your decor, or it can transport you to realms beyond and into the immense and exciting world of plants.

Rows of cheerful, blooming netted iris *(Iris reticulata)* and forsythia branches dispel lingering winter weather that confines the gardener indoors.

integrating garden and decor

Tending an indoor garden is not the same as turning a spade in an outdoor plot, yet here, too, is a blend of art and science. Artistry indoors involves a sensitive and knowing execution that must also take into account the setting and furnishings. There are some constraints that go along with a gardener's freehand approach, and success depends on following time-tested rules that pertain to living flora wherever it grows.

More and more plants are finding their way indoors, as plant lovers reach beyond the traditional house-plant to a broader sense of "garden." To some extent, there has been a loss of interest in timeworn tropicals and a yearning to experiment with less familiar species. Many gardeners-at-heart simply want to surround themselves with living, growing plants and bring inside the treasures they love.

Here is not only a horticultural challenge, but a decorating one as well. Which plants thrive indoors, how do they blend in, and where will the garden grow best? Answering those questions can prompt you to take a look at your interiors in a new light. Suddenly, there are unusual shapes and textures to blend with existing furnishings, new ways to combine accessories, and a reshuffling of space to house living plants. A broader color spectrum appears, and each plant offers unique decorative possibilities. But it behooves the gardener to weigh artistic advantages against horticultural needs. After all, we want our gardens to grow.

SHOWCASING SPECIMENS

The comfortable ambience that living plants radiate has become an almost indispensable element in home decorating. Many people rely on an indoor garden for an attention-getting prod at tired decor and to produce fresh sparks to ignite dull days. Although it's possible to assemble a garden simply for a shocking effect, in the long run it makes more sense that it be a clear expression of your own personal style, a message you want to see and hear day in and day out. A bold, dramatic plant combination, for instance, is unmistakably eye-catching, but it's also more fitting in a spare contemporary setting than in a country motif where kitchen herbs, forced bulbs, or an encased tropical garden would fit in seamlessly.

Don't be reluctant to take risks, though, and to flaunt the unusual. Pull your prized creations out of the corner into open space where they'll create a stir. Feature an oversized basket of orchids prominently on a low table. Without fail, it will dazzle, whereas a jumble of several small containers creates no impact at all.

Space alone may be the deciding factor in how you display your indoor garden. In close quarters, look for open shelves and corners on a sideboard; convert a stool or inverted pot into a tabletop; gather together a garden in a tray for a bathroom vanity. Certain parameters may guide you toward placing an herb topiary near the chopping block or a dish garden as a dining table centerpiece.

Your final decision on where to display your garden ultimately rests with your own eye — that is, in whatever site pleases you most. At the same time, you'll want the garden to look its best, and it will if you make every attempt to meet each plant's needs. Be prepared to acknowledge that where you choose to display your garden may not be where it should reside for most of the year. There is no way to escape the need for proper light, temperature, and humidity, which often limits where plants will thrive indoors.

Garden Showcase
Humidity-loving orchids showcase beautifully in open glass containers. A layer of gravel lifts plants above excess moisture, and the glass admits light, promotes humidity, and shows off plants under sparkling conditions.

CREATING
A GARDEN ROOM

Enthusiastic gardeners fashion rooms within the outdoor landscape and decorate them for pleasure and relaxation. Inside the home, the reverse is possible – that is, a re-creation of a garden atmosphere in a room dedicated entirely to plants, filled with casual furnishings, outdoorsy paraphernalia, and whatever imbues an enclosed space with the captivating vitality of the garden.

Of course, it isn't necessary or even possible for most people to dedicate an entire room to a garden, but many homes have a summer porch or an enclosed breezeway that could serve the same purpose.

The most exquisite rooms are glassed-in interiors or additions to the house with garden views that dissolve the barrier between indoors and out. Although an outside view may not be possible in a particular room, one will develop soon enough inside. Light patterns, tables, and seating areas organize space automatically, making way for new specimens as your garden grows.

The most dominant feature in a garden room is natural light that bathes foliage and shines on every possible nook and cranny, tempting you to fill them with plants. Although bountiful exposure to sun is the main purpose of a garden room, you may end up with too much of a good thing. Unrelenting rays in any season spell disaster for tender, shade-loving foliage and may cause temperatures to soar beyond comfort. How you shade and diffuse light should be planned from the very beginning, along with other critical concerns such as heat, water supply, and drainage. Durable flooring is also essential, preferably one made of stone or tile to withstand the routines of gardening.

Garden rooms constructed solely out of weather-resilient materials offer the same potential as a greenhouse for high humidity and warm temperatures. A room that serves multiple purposes, such as a sitting room or a dining alcove, however, imposes critical restrictions on moisture levels. Depending on the furnishings you have, your garden space may welcome more Mediterranean and desert-climate species than tropicals.

Ultimately, the garden room is an expression of your own personality and shouldn't be severely limited by either plant combinations or furnishings. You may want to depart from the design motifs in other rooms and introduce earth tones of adobe tan and terra-cotta, a shocking palette, or something antique or classical.

Above all, make the room your own, outfitting it as a comfortable retreat where easy-care wicker or contemporary metal invites you to stay and commune with plants and fragrances of the garden.

Giant tropical bananas, vibrant bougainvillea vines, and a tabletop citrus defy the seasons in a year-round garden room.

Bright, diffused light is essential for indoor gardens. Ryegrass and an oncidium orchid bask in this bathroom in the photo below. On the facing page, herbs flourish best when full sun streams through windows for at least 4 hours a day.

SUNROOMS

A sunroom is more versatile in a household than is a full-scale garden room. It warmly receives family and garden and is ideal for rejuvenating plants. The flooring and furnishings must be protected from water damage, but plants repay your efforts by releasing oxygen into the air and freshening the atmosphere. Move plants here to expose them to sunlight missing from dimmer interiors. Once they recoup their prime condition, move them back into view on a tabletop.

KITCHENS AND BATHS

In some homes, the kitchen is never without a sprig of some plant rooting in a miniature garden on the windowsill. Humidity tends to build up more in kitchens, which has great benefits because it fosters plant life. Windows are where light is brightest, but there are other hospitable sites. Herbs and succulents, common to kitchens, will grow for short periods on open shelves and countertops.

Pay close attention to the herbs in your kitchen garden, for these are sun lovers that fail fast when out of their element. You'll be much happier with their overall performance when you have at least one, if not two, backup herb gardens that you can rotate in and out of the kitchen. After a month or so indoors, many herbs are depleted of the foliage that made them so attractive in the first place. With a move outdoors to speed their

without worrying about spills or mishaps. If such a space is large enough, it can also serve as a recovery zone when interior light is dim and indoor heat is either too high or too low.

With the change in seasons, you may need to relocate plants as indoor temperatures and light levels fluctuate. In winter, watch out for drafts in an entry, in an uninsulated sunroom, and along outside walls, where you may not feel the cold air to which plants respond. Although some tropical orchids and cacti need a lower nighttime temperature to induce bloom, many foliage plants develop leaf spots when room conditions fluctuate, and some turn black overnight if the thermostat drops below 55°F.

Changes in light patterns thrown by the variations in the angle of the sun from season to season also have an impact on plants. More sun actually streams through windows in winter, when the sun is closer to the horizon, than when it is high overhead in summer, and undiffused winter rays are strong enough to burn foliage.

recovery during the growing season, you'll be able to bring them back in when their substitutes are ready to move out.

It's a common notion that a bathroom is an ideal home for plants that love humidity, and while this is true to some extent, the crux is the availability of sufficient light. Before setting up a bathroom garden, consider whether temperature variability is acceptable. Some people keep the bathroom unheated when they're away for most of the day.

THE INDOOR HABITAT

Some indoor gardens are short-lived; others grow for years. To avoid disappointments, define your expectations before you install a garden. Keep in mind that when you bring certain species indoors, you may be pushing nature beyond its normal limits. Yet most plants can adapt if you ease them into a comfortable niche on a tabletop.

To smooth the transition from outdoors, look for a temporary shelter, one that can be a home away from home for plants during dormancy or when they need a change in conditions. Let plants rest on a cool porch, for example, before you move them from an outdoor nursery into dry heat or air-conditioning and dimmer or artificial light. Plants straight from a steamy greenhouse need the same kind of transition.

A holding area for plants can double as a work site where you change pots, water, and fertilize

preventing water stains

Kitchens and baths have no shortage of water-resistant surfaces, but you'll need to take precautions in other rooms to prevent water stains on tabletops. Plants complement fine furniture beautifully, but once marred, shelves and tables never recover without painstaking refinishing. Impermeable protectors should be as much a part of the garden as the containers themselves. Inspect every mat or trivet you use. Never trust tile or stone or any saucer without first sealing the underside and fitting it with a self-adherent felt pad to prevent scratches.

creative containers

Choosing containers is almost as much fun as growing the garden. The most important factor is the degree to which a pot holds water, because overwatering kills more indoor plants than any other factor. In terms of decor, pot and plant work in tandem from the very beginning to establish the indoor environment. Containers become the hardscape that defines and complements a plant's natural form.

Except for those growing in water, gardens in deep glass containers like the ones on the facing page should be treated as you would a terrarium. A range of styles, as shown in the photo above, makes it easy to coordinate pots with room decor and foliage color. Match pot sizes to rootballs; too much soil in a too-large pot retains moisture for long periods and rots roots.

The overwhelming concern when choosing a container is how it will affect the plants growing in it. Containers with drainage forestall problems from saturated soil and should have a drip saucer. Porous clay pots allow beneficial air circulation and also release excess salt buildup from fertilizers. But all clay pots are not created equal. Once glazed in bright colors, they take on decorative advantages but lose porosity and retain water for longer periods. The increased moisture cuts down on watering frequency and suits some species perfectly but causes decline in others.

ORNAMENTAL CACHEPOTS

Plastic is the most prevalent nonporous container material and the one most plants are familiar with from the nursery. There is nothing wrong with leaving a plant just as you bought it, but, of course, it becomes a great deal more appealing as soon as it's lodged in a cachepot.

Here may lie your preferred approach, for it's far easier to adapt a container to your decor and far more conducive to plant health when you don't plant directly in a drainless pot. Whether you choose a pedestaled urn, copper tub, thrown pot, or fluted seashell, you'll find it easy and convenient to sink one or several plastic pots inside, camouflage them with sphagnum moss, and be finished in an instant.

Dish and tray gardens are somewhat of an exception. Many appealing containers are quite shallow and intended for purposes other than planting a garden. Using them calls for vigilance to avoid overwatering. Some dish gardens, however, are intended to be short-term projects, in which case you needn't be concerned about long-term effects.

BALANCING DESIGN AND FUNCTION

When you enter a room and are immediately drawn to a garden growing there, chances are that its placement shares at least half the credit for its visual impact. An important feature is where the container is placed and what is surrounding it. In addition, quite plain containers can be just as exciting as those with unusual finishes or grand proportions when accessories are used either inside the container or next to it and become part of the architecture of the garden.

Once your garden is in place, take visual cues from its surroundings to adjust proportions of plant to container, garden to room. New plantings often reveal a low profile and benefit from artificial height. You may find that a simple vertical accessory is just what you need for a finishing touch. A pillar or topiary obelisk that supports a vine may be the answer, or it could be something as ordinary as a twisted branchlet blown free by the wind.

In terms of props and accessories, anything goes indoors – conventional or eccentric, simple or elaborate – just as it does in the unfenced garden plot, as long as there's some aesthetic advantage. Serendipitous finds and seasonal touches do well for an informal style. More stylized designs employ artful glass, stones, or candles.

Accessories change year to year, decade to decade. Depending on the effect you want to establish, it may be time to assign a dated collection of wicker baskets to the vegetable garden and invest in new metallic finishes, pale ceramics, or glossy lacquers.

Below, a welded wire sphere brandishing a rusted patina accents an oversized container; it can provide support for a floppy, frolicking vine, such as passionflower (*Passiflora*) or pink jasmine (*Jasminum polyanthum*). On the facing page, a highly polished surface reflects muted light over unfurling fern fronds and brightens an otherwise dim corner.

adapting a bookcase

Open shelves in bookcases away from windows generally receive light intensities too low for plants. To improve conditions, install fluorescent tubes out of sight under shelving as close as 6 inches to flowering species, but never more than 18 to 24 inches away from any plant. Full-spectrum bulbs are most effective. Use a power drill to make an opening in back to access an outlet. Experiment to determine how long to run lights, beginning with 6 to 8 hours a day. Leggy growth indicates too little exposure; bunched foliage, too much. A timer maintains regularity. See page 143 for design ideas.

CAPTURING LIGHT

Without adequate light, plants languish no matter what we do to nurture them. Yet too often we're reluctant to admit that where we want the garden to grow indoors is less than an optimal site. The simplest solution is to reposition tables to capture light where and when your garden needs it. If that isn't possible, try setting plants on a stool or rack placed in front of a window.

There are also a few tricks that manipulate light, increasing a plant's tolerance for an otherwise dim spot. One is to position a mirror or other highly reflective surface behind plants to scatter light throughout the foliage. You'll have to monitor the sun's angle from month to month to guard against dangerously mirrored rays, and possibly move the mirror to different positions to redirect light as the seasons change.

Another approach is to use spot lamps or fluorescent tubes to supplement natural light. Fluorescence is best confined to dedicated racks or underneath shelving. Spot lighting is a little complicated to install but may already be in use in your household, just calling for a garden to move in underneath. Consider using a temporary spot if light is a problem for only a few months of the year.

know your plants

Success with any garden begins before you ever bring a plant home from the nursery. Although many will survive, only those plants whose light, water, fertilizer, temperature, humidity, and potting requirements are met will thrive. Read plant tags, ask questions, and bolster your determination to heed answers as you build and maintain your garden.

Along with good looks, a garden's growth is a good indicator of its health and vigor. Many species desirable for indoor gardens grow extremely slowly and remain compact. Changes in this natural habit – sparse foliage, for example – indicate that something is amiss, such as light or fertility. It takes a bit of sleuthing to determine exactly what is wrong, but first you must recognize the warning signs.

Fast-growing plants must be confined to a limited space, though plants with excessively rampant growth should never be introduced indoors in the first place. Learn what a plant's tolerance is for pinching and pruning before you take drastic steps, because each species is different. All plants depend on their foliage for sustenance, and many are severely shocked when it's lost.

MINI ENVIRONMENTS

Special plants call for special care indoors. Sometimes that means constructing an environment to warm tender foliage, increase light, or raise humidity. A terrarium provides such care, as do full-spectrum lights and humidity trays.

Grouping pots is one way to meet special needs, as long as there is ample air circulation. Masses of foliage trap and concentrate humid-

ity that forms as moisture evaporates. Closely grouped plants intensify the garden effect and make watering rounds easier.

Glass covers serve the same purpose and are especially useful for individual plants. But here, too, lies a risk of excess moisture being held too long without air movement. Lift cloches daily or, better yet, support them an inch or two above the table, but watch for moisture that drips from the glass.

WINDOW GARDENS

Lacking a garden room or a sunroom, homes with a greenhouse window are able to create even larger mini environments. A woven shade on the outside and a more decorative one on the inside are usually required to protect against too much sun as well as heat loss, but they can be raised when opposite conditions are needed. A dish of water supplies humidity and side vents allow for cross ventilation.

On the facing page, clustered plants share humidity as water vapor rises from their foliage. A little distance among pots allows for good air circulation. A glass cloche, such as the one above, preserves essential high humidity for flamingo flower (*Anthurium*). At left, shimmering tints on orange New Zealand sedge (*Carex testacea*) depend on moist soil and regular exposure to direct sun. In less intense light, olive green foliage predominates.

tray & dish gardens

Gardening often begins as an idea inspired by the shape of a leaf, the color of foliage, or the promise of an exquisite blossom. Indoor gardening is no different, though sometimes a striking container ignites a desire to dabble in that age-old blend of art and science. Although indoor gardening prohibits laying out elaborate design schemes in borders and parterres, tray and dish gardens provide a setting for simple yet impressive patterns. Small-scale interior landscapes challenge our creativity and yield exciting plant combinations that are often impossible outdoors. These gardens express a unique blend of earthiness and style while remaining easy to assemble and maintain. They feature small, shallow-rooted plants that give a garden a low profile – perfect for a tabletop.

garden mosaic

This is a garden bed in miniature, where a checkerboard mosaic of creeping mint and river stones connects you to the natural world all the while you're indoors. Like any constantly growing garden, this one calls to an appreciative eye to watch it grow, a green thumb to snip back stray stems, and a nose to enjoy the spicy fragrance of freshly cut leaves.

Polished stones impart a clean, uncluttered look to this dish garden, reflecting a sense of tidiness and order. A minimalist approach restricts the foliage to a simple creeping mint ground cover, but the result becomes an artistic, undemanding element in a room's decor.

Because geometry is the essential element in this design, place your garden mosaic where it will harmonize with its surroundings. It is best suited to a room with pared-down accessories, where the sharp, artful contrasts within its sleek, sparse form will stand out.

- Bright, direct or indirect light
- Even moisture
- Cool temperature
- Replace plants annually or as needed

Although there's nothing fussy about the minimal color, texture, and intricacy here, you'll have fun collecting and putting together the component materials that suit your gardening and decorating style.

WHAT YOU'LL NEED

Thickly growing creeping Corsican mint (Mentha requienii)

Sharp knife

Scissors or garden shears

Soilless potting mix

Distilled water

Small trowel or large spoon

Low rectangular container, 2–3 inches deep

Slow-release fertilizer

Polished river stones, thin and flat

ONGOING CARE

Water only when top half of soil under stones feels dry to the touch, and then only with distilled water. Hard water leaves a residue; chemically treated water harms plants. Trim fast-growing plants every week or two; trim slow-growing species every other month, or as needed.

Begin by making a scale drawing of the mosaic you want to create. Then select a color palette for the container and stones so your garden will blend with other accessories in the room. Ideally, your container should have drainage holes and rest on a tray so that the plants never sit in water. Garden shops, pet stores, and landscape suppliers carry a wide variety of stones in dark hues, earth tones, and bright pastels.

Using a sharp knife, cut large blocks of mint into 2- to 3-inch plugs. Switch to scissors or garden shears to trim away matted roots and finish edges squarely.

Moisten potting mix with distilled water. Using a trowel, fill container with potting mix to within ½ inch of the top and apply a half dose of slow-release fertilizer.

Set in plugs of mint and gently firm potting mix around roots. Lay stones neatly among plugs, covering soil completely.

When plant vigor declines, after a year or more, empty and clean the container, then rebuild the garden with new plants.

Don't be afraid to improvise as you build your garden. Instead of stones, try using delicate seashells from a coastal stroll or a pocketful of pebbles collected on a summer's day.

You aren't limited, either, by plant choices. Alternatives range from fast-growing baby's tears (Soleirolia soleirolii), to more moderately paced woolly or elfin thyme (Thymus pseudolanuginosus or T. serpyllum 'Elfin') and Scotch or Irish moss (Sagina subulata), to a slow-growing mini mondo grass (Ophiopogon japonicus) such as 'Kyoto Dwarf'.

Cut and Trim

Plugs 2 to 3 inches square work best and are easiest to cut, though you may want to create a pattern of diamonds, circles, or other shapes. Depending on the size and configuration of your mosaic, purchase plants in 6-packs, 4-inch pots, or flats.

creative mulch choices

Mulch in any garden slows evaporation from the soil and reduces the frequency of watering. But in a garden mosaic, its role is as decorative as it is practical. The mulch you choose establishes the overriding mood of a dish garden, whether it's formal and precise in neutral colors with smooth, level textures or less meticulously drawn with coarser textures and arresting colors.

Clockwise from lower left: Sharp sand, polished river stones, opaque beach glass, textured terra-cotta balls, and aquarium gravel are all good choices. Buy materials for decorative mulches at a garden center, a florist, or an aquarium shop. Clean and rinse beach glass repeatedly to remove salt residue.

succulent collection and desert garden

What could be better than a garden that takes care of itself? For today's busy gardener, a collection of succulents and cacti keeps the garden growing indoors despite periods of neglect. These water-conserving plants flourish with very little attention and manage to stay on schedule, producing eye-popping blooms. Some species send up a stalk of dangling bells; others sport a wreath of lively, daisy-like flowers around their crowns. With just a bit of encouragement from regular care, most types slowly spread into attractive clumps, generating offspring around the base to join in the show.

Succulents, such as the ones at left, have evolved around the globe with this easygoing style. In their native habitats, many species survive for long periods by relying on water stored in moisture-laden stems, leaves, and roots. When water is available, they stock up for dry days ahead.

- Very bright light
- Moister in summer, drier in winter
- Warm days, cool nights
- Long-lived

Of the thousands of cacti and succulents, many become tree size, while others remain minuscule. Select those that won't grow out of bounds and will complement the container of your choice. Stemless globes, rosettes, mat-forming clumps, and short columnar forms are best suited to indoor gardens. Grow them singly in shallow pots and group the containers, or craft a community in a broad, flat dish.

WHAT YOU'LL NEED

Compatible group of mixed cacti or succulents

Shallow container, 2–4 inches deep

Trowel

Cactus soil mix

Horticultural sand (optional)

Gravel mulch (optional)

Distilled water or rainwater

Balanced fertilizer

Spray bottle

ONGOING CARE

Allow soil mix to dry completely before watering, then give it a good soaking and allow water to drain. For pots with no drainage holes, water only until the soil is moist throughout. Standing water will cause plants to rot. Fertilize lightly in summer or succulents will lose their form and become lanky.

Tabletops are ideal places to feature unusual plants, and succulents especially are best viewed from above. *Crassula, Sedum, Sempervivum,* and *Echeveria* species and their numerous hybrids offer seemingly limitless varieties from which to choose. Although you won't want to touch cactus spines, you'll appreciate the diversity of their forms when you see them at eye level.

Easy care and long life are hallmarks of succulents and cacti – if their basic requirements are met. Make sure that species planted in the same container have similar growth habits and cultural needs. Your composition will be most appealing when you balance rigid and spiky forms with leafy and globular shapes.

If you opt for spiny cacti, handle them with care! Wrap plants with folded newspaper or use kitchen tongs when potting and moving them.

Cactus soil mix provides needed porosity, but be alert to brand variations. Mix in gritty horticultural sand – never beach sand – if drainage appears slow. A topdressing of gravel helps keep cacti dry.

An east-facing window will suit nearly all plants, though desert cacti can take a southern exposure. For balanced growth, turn containers regularly so that light strikes all sides. A bay or garden window is ideal for overhead light, but in all cases, be prepared to shield plants if sunlight is so strong that they will burn.

During the growing season, plants require a surprising amount of water and regular fertilizing. The caution here is never to water until the soil dries out completely. Rainwater, if you can collect it, or distilled water, is best.

Most cacti and succulents enter a resting phase from late October until spring, often after flowering. Many types will survive with no water during that time, but to prevent shriveling, mist or moisten soil lightly about once a month. Low nighttime temperatures help them rest.

Leave small offsets intact at the base of succulents until plants become too crowded, then thin only enough to allow space for future growth. Pot up young offsets in small containers until an ample root mass develops and they're ready for a new dish garden. Best color develops in bright light and in winter when little moisture is applied.

succulent garden plants

▼ Rosette-Forming Succulents

These species are among the most charming and colorful succulents. Mix and match subtle blends of frosty blue and pinkish white, dark and lime green, and cultivars flushed purple or bronze, such as the pointy-leafed *Echeveria* 'Black Prince' shown at right.

▲ Window Plant

This window plant *(Haworthia cymbiformis)* is a bubbly rosette that reveals dark green striations throughout turgid, translucent leaves. Place it out of direct sun in moderate to bright light.

Desert Grouping

Garden and art blend seamlessly when dramatic plants, such as columnar cacti with sculptural qualities, are grouped together.

▼ Blue cereus

Easy-to-grow powder blue cereus (*Stenocereus pruinosus*) is a dramatic species whose beauty emanates from the powdery coating on otherwise dull green stems. Stout, sharp spines line fluted ribs and stand in colorful contrast to the shadowy blue skin. A small container will restrict growth for many years well below its 10- to 20-foot potential.

▲ Organ-pipe cactus

The organ-pipe cactus (*Stenocereus thurberi*) develops many tall, upright, bluish green stems in desert regions, but its height and spread are severely restricted in a container. In youth, glossy spines and prominent chestnut brown hairs line dark green stems. Flowers appear only on taller, mature plants.

desert garden plants

◄ Bunny-ears

So named for its rounded, yellowish green pads, bunny-ears *(Opuntia microdasys)* is a favorite of indoor gardeners. Lacking characteristic spines, this cactus is dotted with colorful, velvety tufts called glochids, tiny bristles that should nevert be touched because they are irritating to the skin. Depending on the variety, glochids are yellow, white, or cinnamon.

► Balloon cactus

The ribs of balloon cactus *(Parodia magnifica,* syn. *Notocactus magnificus)* are filled with thin, flexible spines that give this species its bright outline. Bluish green stems elongate to 12 inches over many years, all the while producing offsets around the base. Large sulfur-yellow flowers about 2 inches in diameter appear around the crown.

centerpiece garden

Indoor gardens spark magic everywhere that people gather, but when living plants grace a dining room, they create an especially distinctive atmosphere. Fresh color and fragrance never fail to enliven an ordinary family meal or suggest a relaxed yet elegant setting for a festive occasion.

A garden centerpiece anchors your table setting and assumes its proper role only when it doesn't intrusively interrupt a line of sight or the flow of conversation. The low trays of early-blooming iris in this tabletop garden are a perfect center attraction. Their bulbs grow to blossoming perfection in very little soil and fit handily in shallow trays. Iris in the Reticulata group are small, delicate plants nearly always under 8 inches tall. Their grasslike foliage is slimmer than that of the more common bearded iris and often appears after flowering.

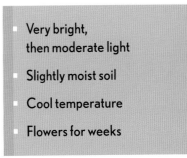

- Very bright, then moderate light
- Slightly moist soil
- Cool temperature
- Flowers for weeks

Although blooming bulbs are lovely, when crowded in a container their stems appear awkward at the base unless they're masked by foliage. A thick covering, such as a ferny selaginella, sometimes called spike moss, fills in beautifully, balances the taller bulbs, and retains moisture. The most common selaginellas add a complementary chartreuse or bright green color and, though they are only 1 to 2 inches tall, their foliage drapes attractively over the edges of a container. To round out the display, sprays of early-blooming forsythia lend a sunny air.

WHAT YOU'LL NEED

Netted iris *(Iris reticulata)* bulbs

Spike moss *(Selaginella)*

2- to 3-inch-deep container

Small trowel

Potting soil

2 or 3 empty 2-inch containers

ONGOING CARE

If your tray has no drainage holes, water sparingly but keep soil evenly moist. Snip off flowers as they fade. To extend blooming period, set outside (in mild climates) or in a cool spot to rest overnight.

You can create an instant garden by purchasing bulbs in bloom and setting them in trays with a ground cover. Avid gardeners who have storage space may want to try their hand at forcing bulbs (see page 126).

Begin in autumn for blooms in late winter. Choose large or top-size bulbs for the largest possible blossoms, smaller bulbs for more compact growth and individual blooms. Select a container twice the depth of the bulbs to allow for root growth.

Fill trays half full with potting mix and set in bulbs so they are nearly touching. Position an empty 2-inch container in two or three places to reserve a planting well for a ground cover to be added later, then continue adding soil to within 1/2 inch of the rim.

Water just enough to lightly moisten and settle the soil. Cover the container loosely with plastic and store in an old refrigerator set between 35 and 50°F or in a cool, out of the way, protected outdoor site for about three months. Lift the cover every few weeks to circulate air and check for moisture. To bloom well, these hardy bulbs must stay cool and never dry out completely.

In three months, check for hints of growth. When pale shoots emerge, move the container to a milder location out of direct sun. Plant selaginella in the reserved wells and begin watering your garden. In a week, move it to a warmer, sunny spot.

In another three or four weeks, when flower buds appear, move the container to its final spot, but out of direct sun.

Spike Moss

Mosslike and ferny, selaginella prefers moderate to bright light, a humid atmosphere, and average fertility. Frequent misting keeps foliage soft and lush. Alternatively, choose English ivy, baby's tears, other types of moss, or even a dwarf grape ivy vine *(Cissus striata)* as a ground cover.

candle centerpiece

No need to stop gardening after the flowers fade. Keep your centerpiece growing but substitute the ambience of candlelight for blossoms and establish a whole new mood. Before placing a candle in the container, trim iris foliage at the soil line, invert the garden onto newspaper, and pull out bulbs from the bottom and discard. Rearrange the selaginella around the candle.

water gardens

Winter or summer, indoor water gardens mesmerize and fascinate. Like an underwater scene in a tropical sea at dusk, they reveal seductive, ghostly visions. Water gardens can be bold and elaborate and demand frequent attention or remain quite simple, surviving on their own for weeks at a time. Some of the most streamlined contain only one or two plants chosen for their alluring sculptural effects. As feathery roots of submerged plants unfurl, they steal the show as dancers in a tall glass vase. If your idea of a water feature includes the calming effect of bubbling water from a fountain, you can have that too, even in the limited space of a tabletop.

floating garden

A miniature floating garden takes little time to create, but to arrive at a pleasing composition, you'll want to consider shape and texture of both container and plant, as well as how light plays off the water and glass. The effect is most spectacular when neither your container nor your tabletop is crowded and your garden appears as a center of serenity.

Choose from a wide assortment of marginal and aquatic plants with neat, compact habits. Many have graceful, wispy root systems that are beautifully revealed in clear, vertical containers. In deep water, swirling submerged plants not only create a visual spectacle, but they also promote the health of a water garden by releasing oxygen and reducing the growth of algae.

In the garden at left, rosettes of floating and aerial leaves on the buoyant, inflated stems of water hyacinth (*Eichhornia crassipes*) conspire to create an exotic indoor waterscape. The long, purplish roots dangle gracefully as much as 12 inches in a deep container. With adequate light, violet-blue flowers borne on spikes appear. Take care that plants never find their way to outdoor pools, where they become noxious weeds and may even be illegal in some regions.

Alternatively, tall, spiraling leaves of eelgrass (*Vallisneria spiralis*), fine feathery lengths of hornwort (*Ceratophyllum demersum*), and dark green whorls of Canadian pond-weed (*Elodea canadensis*) are other underwater options. Fernlike fairy moss (*Azolla caroliniana*), frogbit (*Hydrocharis morsus-ranae*), and water lettuce (*Pistia stratiotes*) make good floaters. Look for these plants at pet stores and pond nurseries.

- Bright, indirect light
- Distilled water or rainwater
- Average room temperature
- Long-lived above 55°F

Like other species, water plants may experience a briefer life span indoors than in open air. Those native to pond-margin habitats, such as marsh marigold (*Caltha palustris*) and sweet flag (*Acorus gramineus*), will be longer-lived if you move them outdoors for several weeks during warm weather. (See pages 40 and 50 for details on caring for a water garden.)

◄ Floral Floaters

Pure white camellia petals rise in striking contrast to an underlayer of floating common duckweed (*Lemna minor*) in a stylish ceramic dish. A single, casual blossom captures the essence of the garden spirit, extending the outdoor experience to a tabletop. Although a flower fades within a few days or weeks, memories of the garden where it was gathered linger on.

Rainwater or distilled water at room temperature supports the longest life, but it also helps to recut the stem before floating a blossom.

◄ Synchronized Swimming

Texture and light underscore the beauty of a floating marsh marigold (*Caltha palustris*) and submerged grassy-leafed sweet flag (*Acorus gramineus*) in a condensed version of a pond garden, shown on the facing page. These very different genera marry well in a tall glass vase. Each will reach from 6 to 15 inches in height and slowly sprout new foliage from the base.

To create the garden, mix 1 or 2 tablespoons of crushed charcoal with a thin layer of gravel to anchor roots after you set plants in the vase. Fill with rainwater or distilled water; add a tablet of water-garden fertilizer, following label directions. When you change the water, pour it through a colander to catch the gravel. A mild algicide formulated for only indoor use can be added to large floating gardens that receive direct sun.

tropical garden

Many tender plants that have proved reliable indoors can be grown in water as easily as in soil. You may have already sprouted a tropical water garden when you rooted cuttings of your favorite houseplants and left them growing on the windowsill. Take these same plants (or a wide range of others), place them in a dynamite vase on a tabletop, and you have the beginnings of a garden room.

Although neither is a true grass, the two grasslike plants in this delightful garden have a natural affinity for shallow water and grow best when their feet are always wet. Leaves radiating like umbrella ribs atop arching, angled stems bestow *Cyperus alternifolius* with the common name umbrella plant. The display is striking in full light, but in a dim room, under a modest spotlight, it creates unparalled shadow patterns and a spidery silhouette. Because no foliage develops low on umbrella plant stems, a ring of finely textured grassy-leafed sweet

- Bright, filtered light
- Distilled water or rainwater
- Average room temperature, slightly cooler at night
- Long-lived with routine care

flag *(Acorus gramineus)* is fitted neatly around the base to imbue an open, airy feel and complete the garden. Bright chips of sea glass fill the bottom of the water reservoir, casting a contemporary look.

Alternatively, dwarf sweet flags are only 4 to 6 inches tall. Their sword-shaped leaves nestle in a container in short, fanlike sprays. Where space is at a premium, select dwarf umbrella plant (*Cyperus alternifolius* 'Gracilis' or 'Nana'), which stays under 18 inches tall.

WHAT YOU'LL NEED

Umbrella plant (*Cyperus alternifolius* 'Gracilis' or 'Nana')

Sweet flag *(Acorus gramineus)*, green or variegated

Rainwater or distilled water

Fertilizer tablets

Glass or ceramic container, 6 inches deep

Sea glass or other anchoring material

Crushed charcoal (optional)

pH test strips

ONGOING CARE

Maintain water level 3 to 4 inches above root mass. Fertilize every month from late spring through summer with fertilizer made for water gardens. When water appears murky, rinse roots and clean the container. After three to four years, separate clumps when they become crowded.

Let the size of your container determine how large your tropical water garden will grow. Where there is ample room for root development, umbrella plant can reach 3 feet in height and spread half as wide. When not crowded, sweet flag's rhizomes enlarge at the water's surface and produce increasing numbers of finely tapered, grasslike blades that fan into arching sprays.

If you purchase plants growing in soil, clean and rinse roots and rhizomes carefully to avoid breakage. Let them soak temporarily to loosen any soil particles that tend to cling.

Both plant species featured here thrive in shallow water about 4 inches deep; sweet flag can be submerged as long as water temperature stays below 72°F.

Well-developed root systems require little support, but young plants stand upright more readily when securely anchored in a support medium. Sea glass, coarse gravel, stones, tile or terra-cotta chips, and glass marbles are just a few suggestions, but you'll want to choose whatever is most harmonious with your decor.

A layer of crushed charcoal in the bottom helps keep water clean. If algae regularly develop, consider adding another submerged plant to oxygenate the water (see page 35).

If foliage on your umbrella plant develops brown tips, check the pH of the water for neutrality. To alter acidity, add a pinch of baking soda; decrease alkalinity with vinegar. Always test carefully, however, that water is neutral before refilling your water garden. You can purchase a testing tape from a hardware or pool-supply store or garden center.

Umbrella Plant

At once both stylish and playful, umbrella plant (also sometimes called umbrella grass) casts interesting patterns as light passes through foliage clusters. Its relative dwarf papyrus (*Cyperus profiler*) produces grasslike tufts, as well as umbrella-style spikelets.

tropical garden plants

◄ Sweet flag

Tufts of grassy-leafed sweet flag *(Acorus gramineus)* make themselves at home in a water garden. The species plant bears dark green, glossy leaves about ½ inch wide and 6 to 12 inches long. The cultivar 'Variegatus' is marked with creamy white stripes on slightly narrower leaves. When either the leaves or the rhizomes are bruised, a sweet fragrance is released.

▲ Dracaena

Dracaena cincta (syn. *D. marginata*) resembles a low fountain of striped foliage in its youth, but it becomes quite leggy with age. As the stem elongates, this species — like most dracaenas — grows out of proportion in a tabletop garden and must be shortened. Reposition the top growth in your water garden, taking care to keep foliage above the waterline. Young leaves are 6 to 8 inches long; in maturity, they may reach more than 12 inches in length.

► Belgian evergreen

The graceful nature and slow growth of Belgian evergreen *(Dracaena sanderiana)* make it an appealing subject for small indoor gardens. It resembles a young corn plant with creamy margins, but the similarity ends there. Shiny green, sometimes wavy, leaves are bedecked with ribbons of creamy white along the margins. When the canelike stem grows too tall (it can reach up to 5 feet), simply clip off the top, discard the lower portion, and place the leafy top growth in your water garden to root anew. The leaves grow 6 to 10 inches long. Fertilize with half doses once a month from late spring through summer.

bog garden

Poor drainage is usually considered a liability rather than an asset in gardens, except for plants that prefer boggy conditions. For them and the wildlife they sustain, constant moisture is essential. Although you will have to leave behind the fauna, floral denizens of marshes are handsome plants that you can bring into your home, lifting them from supporting roles in their natural setting to stars in their own right on a tabletop.

The diverse nature of bog plants never fails to fascinate. Some are lush and broad leafed, while others are slim and spiky. Many low ground-cover types grow mainly underwater, with just their tips sprawling over the surface. Indoors, they provide an aesthetic visual balance to an assortment of taller species.

Any waterproof container, from a ceramic pot, to a fish tank, to a dishpan, is suitable for a bog garden. Your choice will depend on where you want to display the garden and how many plants you'd like to grow. If you have any doubts about the compatibility of your choice of plants and container, coat the interior with a sealant or fit it with a liner to prevent any contaminants from leaching into the growing medium. Most bog plants are sensitive to any foreign matter around their roots.

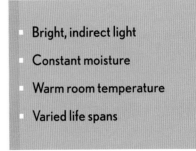

- Bright, indirect light
- Constant moisture
- Warm room temperature
- Varied life spans

4 or 5 species of bog plants

Sphagnum peat moss

Rainwater or distilled water

Bucket or bowl

Washed sand (not beach sand) or perlite

Fine peat moss (optional)

Hand trowel

Waterproof container, about 4 inches deep

Spray bottle

Orchid or acidic plant fertilizer

ONGOING CARE

Sphagnum peat moss holds water for long periods, but you'll need to check the planting mix at least once a week to ensure even moisture. You may find it easiest to sink carnivorous plants in their pots, then lift them out for a rest period in winter, when they prefer drier conditions. Because the high mineral content of hard water is fatal to bog plants, use only rainwater or distilled water.

Bog plants' few basic requirements are very easy to meet. Once they're planted and you're off to a good start, this dynamic version of a water garden is low on maintenance but packed full of fun and surprises. Leafless stems, unusual blooms, dewy foliage, and squiggly growth seem to change from week to week.

A good solid start with a bog garden depends on the planting mix's giving your plants what they need: a reliably moist, acidic environment. Sphagnum peat moss is the most important ingredient.

In a bucket, prepare a mix of equal parts washed sand and shredded sphagnum moss, or equal parts sand, shredded sphagnum moss, and fine peat moss.

Moisten the mix thoroughly, allowing it to stand for several hours if the moss resists wetting. It will be thick and slushy. Meanwhile, moisten the plants in their nursery pots and allow them to drain.

Using a trowel, fill the container to within 1 inch of the top, pressing out air pockets as you work. Loosen plant roots carefully and scoop out a hole that is large enough to accommodate them. Set in plants and lightly press planting mix over roots, then mulch the surface with the moistened shredded sphagnum.

Bog plants require little fertility. A light misting once in spring and once in summer with an orchid or acidic plant product should be sufficient. Reduce the concentration to one fourth or one half of normal.

Bog Conditions

Build your own bog for indoor plants from sphagnum moss mixed with coarse sand and water.

bog garden plants

◄ Mare's-tail

The fine, bright green foliage of mare's-tail (*Hippuris vulgaris*) spreads freely in shallow conditions. Slightly stiff, pinelike foliage cloaks stems that bend as they stand upright or curl along the surface and drape gracefully over the edge of a container. The submerged foliage is finer and oxygenates the water held by the peat moss. All foliage is fragile and more easily broken than it appears.

▼ Sundews

Drosera are as attractive to insects as they are to the gardener! Green leaves on these rosette-forming carnivores are lined with small, sticky tentacles that lie in wait for an unsuspecting gnat or other tiny insect to land and provide nourishment. The colorful *D. capensis*, with its red-tinted tentacles, and the more rounded-leafed *D. aliciae* are particularly recommended for new growers. If you notice that insects are not captured, drop a few dead gnat-sized insects on a leaf two or three times a year.

▲ Cape rush

The stiff, nearly leafless, dark green stems of cape rush (*Chondropetalum tectorum*) radiate from the base of this stunning marsh plant. Growth is slow in a container, preserving an open, airy disposition as a perfect foil to leafier foliage plants. With maturity, clusters of dark brown flowers appear at the stem tips. As stems become crowded or overly long, cut them out one by one at the base.

► Peace lily

Equally at home in a moist or dry environment, peace lily, or white flag (*Spathiphyllum*), decorates indoor gardens with frequent blooms and attractive glossy foliage. Leaves open on long, thin stems rising in clusters from the base. Choose a form that is suited to small-scale indoor gardens, such as *Spathiphyllum* 'Petite' or *S. wallisii*, both of which reach about 12 inches tall.

fountain garden

Close your eyes and visualize a trickling stream whose melodic sounds emanate from your kitchen counter, a table beside an armchair, or the comfort of your patio. Add a collection of plants to your tabletop fountain and you have a garden scene that enlivens the acoustic dimension.

The reservoir in this small tabletop fountain welcomes two young Belgian evergreens (*Dracaena sanderiana*). At the opposite end, water gently bubbles and cascades down an elevated ceramic waterfall in a rhythmic murmur that calls up visions of the great outdoors.

Many fountains designed simply for a quiet murmuring sound or to show off a collection of river stones or seashells can be arranged to accommodate plants, too. Or you can create your own Japanese-style *tsukubai* fountain out of a shallow ceramic bowl, a submersible pump, and a bamboo spout.

Your choice of fountain depends on the type of plants you want to grow.

Conversely, if you already have a fountain, choose plants appropriate to its size. Compact water plants and dwarf species are most suitable to a fountain garden, though cuttings of larger plants can also be used. A good place to find small water plants is at a pet store or wherever aquarium supplies are sold.

Buy plants bare root or wash away all traces of soil from potted plants. Anchor them in the bottom of the fountain reservoir on top of 1 or 2 tablespoons of crushed charcoal and cover them with pea or aquarium gravel. Add a few larger pieces of decorative rock to hold the gravel in place. (See pages 40 and 50 for details on caring for a water garden.)

- Bright, indirect light
- Distilled water
- Room temperature
- Replace plants as they outgrow fountain reservoir

sculpture garden

Few gardens are as instantly complete as a simple water garden. Within minutes of bringing a plant into your home, you can sit back and admire not only your own handiwork but nature's exquisite artistry as well.

A host of plants grow in a garden medium reduced to its simplest form: a glass of water. But a discerning eye and an inventive impulse can quickly transform the growing site to suit your decorating style. Clear and colored glass are some of the best choices for a container, for you'll want to display a plant's striking underwater growth as well as its foliage. Glossy, textured leaves and twisty stems form intriguing sculptural elements in a water garden, but so, too, do delicate roots and bulky rhizomes. Viewed through the clarity of a beautiful glass container, they emerge as key elements in your decorating scheme and serve as living sculpture.

- Bright, indirect light
- Distilled water or rainwater
- Average room temperature
- Varied life spans

Many plants that inhabit outdoor water gardens can be grown indoors, as long as you meet their growth requirements. Dwarf species and compact forms that don't call for long periods of direct sunlight are the most successful. Those with unusual shapes and vibrant colors are the most eye-catching. Here, from left to right, corkscrew rush (*Juncus effusus* 'Spiralis'), Chinese taro *(Alocasia cucullata),* and twisty twigs of willow (*Salix* 'Flame') are minimalist but captivating.

WHAT YOU'LL NEED

Shade-loving water plants

Distilled water or rainwater, at room temperature

Crushed charcoal

Glass containers

Glass marbles or stones (optional)

Fertilizer tablets

ONGOING CARE

Maintain water level to provide roots with ample growing space. Except for submerged plants, never allow foliage to sink beneath the waterline. Rinse roots, as needed, every few weeks if plants are in a clear container and algae grow. Fertilize very lightly every other month with a tablet made for water gardens.

Foliage and roots in your sculpture water garden have the same requirements for oxygen as any other plant. An aeration system may be needed in a large water garden, but a mere change of water solves the problem for plants in vases and small containers.

Plants previously grown in soil often suffer shock that causes some roots to die when relocated to a water garden. Ease the transition by gently removing soil from a new plant and washing off roots in tepid water. Let it rest in water in a sunless spot for several days, then continue to rinse roots every week or two until shocked roots slough away and new roots form.

A ½-inch layer of crushed charcoal in the bottom of the container helps keep water clean. It isn't uncommon for some of the roots to die back as your plant adjusts to its new home.

Submerge glass marbles or stones, if desired, for visual interest.

After several weeks, add a diluted nutrient solution when you change the water. Products tinted pink or blue detract from a clean, sleek appearance, but they can be used.

You may want to pursue another approach and look into hydroponic techniques or simply use nutrients sold for hydroponic gardens. Many plants maintain good health for long periods with no supplements, but fertilizing promotes faster growth.

clean water is essential

The kind of water you use has a major effect on both plants and containers. Pure water keeps your garden vigorous and clear glass shows it off to its best advantage. If you can collect rainwater, your plants will be grateful. Otherwise, depend on distilled rather than tap water.

Added chemicals are the biggest problem with municipal water supplies, but chlorine and fluoride will evaporate from it if you leave a bowl of water sitting out for a few days. Softened water contains salt compounds that won't dissipate and can't be tolerated by plants. Hard water is more tolerable but leaves unsightly deposits inside clear glass.

In bright sun, algae may grow in clear glass containers, requiring weekly rinsing, but you shouldn't need to scrub glass more frequently than every few months. When you do, avoid abrasive cleansers, never use soap, and always rinse thoroughly to remove all residues.

One way to reduce maintenance of glass vases is to grow several plants in a water garden kept out of view in an aquarium tank or a nonglass container. When you're ready for a change of scene, select one or two plants, rinse them well, and place them on display.

sculpture garden plants

◄ Corkscrew rush

The shiny, leafless stems of corkscrew rush (*Juncus effusus* 'Spiralis') coil and twist in wayward spirals and extraordinary patterns. The corkscrew effect is most dramatic when the stems are viewed against a contrasting background or where they can be seen from all sides. Keep the water level 3 to 4 inches deep.

▲ Willow

Bright white, feathery roots grow fast on twisty stems of a 'Scarlet Curls' willow (*Salix* 'Scarlet Curls') branch. When the root mass fills your glass container, cut off the entire stem bottom and let growth begin anew.

◄ Chinese taro

Water-loving Chinese taro (*Alocasia cucullata*) has imposing, tuberlike rhizomes that are as impressive as its glossy, embossed foliage. Choose a container that holds the rhizome out of the water while the long roots dangle below. Avoid contact with sap from the stems; it may cause skin irritation.

gravel gardens

Gardens crammed full of plants are too visually complex to sustain interest and lose their impact fast. But a simplified and carefully organized garden mesmerizes. One place to begin creating such a garden space is in a gravel medium. Gravel becomes an integral part of gardens when hardscape is as pertinent as plant species in the overall design and execution.

Gravel gardens call for plants that are naturally adapted to water environments, because their roots sit in constant moisture while gravel anchors their stems. Any watertight container may be used, but it must withstand the weight of gravel, which becomes surprisingly heavy even in small amounts. Low, horizontal dishes are especially attractive because they expose the textured, rippled surface of stone. Consider proportion, too. For a pleasing effect, a container's size and the table on which it sits must balance the vertical height of the finished garden.

japanese gardenscape

Economy and harmony in this simple grouping evolve from the same spirit evident in Japanese gardens. In all of their many styles, these centuries-old landscapes elicit a balanced calm mirrored in the aesthetic positioning of rocks, plants, and water. Although authenticity need not be strictly followed in designing an indoor gardenscape, the principles should guide you in choosing a container, plants, and hardscape whose features provide both harmony and counterpoint.

The water in this garden sits quietly just beneath or just above the surface of fine gravel, suggesting the shoreline of a quiet lake. Graceful and grasslike, unbranched cylinders of fiber-optic plant (*Eleocharis*) offer subtle contrast with coarser surfaces. The single bog plant evokes a broader scene, one that leads to nearby stones, which give the impression of a rocky island emerging in the distance.

As you design your own miniature landscape, focus on a favorite natural scene or a full-scale garden that you admire. Even a photograph can furnish inspiration.

Once you have an idea in mind, search for a container, such as a Japanese-style ikebana dish, to enclose the scene without dominating it. Gravel lends support to the plant, but, as the garden floor, its color and dimension will determine the overall scale and mood of the finished design.

Let an aesthetic balance of rocks, driftwood, and other ornaments guide you in your selections. Finally, choose a simple, compatible plant to fit into your design, matching as closely as possible the scene in your mind's eye that inspired the garden.

- Bright, direct or indirect light
- Stable water level
- Moderate room temperature
- Trim or replace plant to maintain scale

◄ Focus on Form

Also known as lucky or curly bamboo, the spiraling dracaena at left is a desirable gift in Asian cultures. It is said to attract positive chi energy and bring good luck. Stand one or a bundle of several stems in gravel for a quick and easy arrangement that lasts for many months. Grow in shallow water out of direct sun; add a drop of African violet fertilizer every other week.

► Minimalist Hardscape

At right, three glass balls, symbolic of stone weathered and polished through the ages, stand above overlapping ripples of a figurative sea. In this imitation of the abstract style of a Japanese *karesansui* garden, there are no plants, no distracting elements to disturb a peaceful, meditative, and symbolic journey through the natural world. Maintaining the garden by smoothing and raking a pattern of waves becomes as restful an undertaking as contemplation itself.

child's fairy-tale garden

Children of all ages embark on flights of fancy in gardens. As adults, we yearn to share our magical moments and hope that at some point we will introduce young folk to the joys of gardening. Sometimes we do. But engaging children for the long term may call for a fairy's inspiration.

Few materials, quick assembly, and ease of maintenance are tangible keys in convincing children to ply their hand with plants. It also helps when they have a personal connection to their creation and choose their own ornaments and characters – however unpredictable they may be – to inhabit it.

Here, a Cicely Mary Barker fairy atop an inverted flower pot inside a simple water garden works its magic under a child's watchful eye. Aquarium gravel supports a colorful Belgian evergreen *(Dracaena sanderiana)* and a trailing *Peperomia scandens* 'Variegata'; a tuft of moss nestles at the base of a twisty willow branch.

By building such a simple gravel garden in a glass globe or a small fish tank, children can watch the garden

grow in their own rooms. Aquarium gravel supports small plants and holds whatever objects they add. The clear view makes it easy to tell when the water level needs attention, the only critical maintenance feature.

For a grassier environment, add a few sprigs of dwarf mondo grass *(Ophiopogon japonicus* 'Nanus', 'Minor', or 'Kyoto Dwarf') or dwarf fiber-optic plant *(Isolepis* syn. *Scirpus)*.

In a situation where a dry garden may be more appropriate, substitute a moistened mixture of one part peat and one part sand for water, plant a few small succulents, top with the same aquarium gravel, and water sparingly from spring through fall. The glass globe helps the sand retain needed moisture.

- Bright, indirect light
- Maintain low water level
- Average room temperature
- Long-lived with regular care

herb gardens

Whether you plant pots of parsley and chives, tufts of thyme and lavender, or a wreath of rosemary, herbs combine the decorative and the practical. Culinary herbs bring garden-fresh greenery right onto the kitchen counter or windowsill, and other aromatic herbs add spice to any atmosphere. You'll enjoy using them every day to lift your spirits, jazz up cooking, refresh the bath, and lend a sensory comfort to your life.

An herbal topiary is elegant enough for a formal living room and cosmetic herbs are always welcome in the bath, but it's in the kitchen where you'll enjoy snippets of fresh herbs on a daily basis. It's easy to satisfy cultural preferences when herbs are planted in individual pots. The small scale of such a garden allows it to march along the windowsill and follow the sun.

culinary herbs

Given the wide choice of plants to bring indoors, none suits the kitchen better than culinary herbs. No matter how you use them, fresh herbs are always far more satisfying than what is stored inside the spice cabinet. You'll find that snipping freshly harvested herbs into an omelette or a salad is so simple when they're growing close at hand. Flavor and aroma from pungent foliage easily become kitchen staples.

Individual pots of aromatic herbs, including oregano, thymes, sages, garlic chives, and parsley, fill this kitchen-countertop garden. Convenient to the cook, fresh herbs are always ready for mincing on the chopping block.

By carefully monitoring two key cultural conditions – water and light – you can keep your herb garden growing for many months. All herbs should be exposed to at least 6 hours of sunlight a day. Out of direct sun, they become leggy and disappointing, and large-leafed types with long stems tend to flop over.

Dwarf cultivars and herbs with compact growth habits develop the most attractive shapes and look their best if you pinch off the stem tips frequently. Most tender herbs, such as cilantro, chervil, basil, and even mint, grow best when the soil is constantly moist. However, more pungent, woody-stemmed herbs, including rosemary and thyme, need to dry out between waterings.

You may find you have better success with all your culinary herbs if you grow each species in small, individual pots in a fast-draining, peat-based potting mix and group the pots according to their water needs.

- Direct sun
- Test soil before watering
- Average room temperature
- Prune regularly; replace annually or as needed

basket of mediterranean herbs

Bouquets of herbal textures and tantalizing scents make themselves at home in any kitchen. Spicy aromas of thyme, rosemary, sage, and oregano perfume the air while their subtle flavors please the palate. You can grow herbs strictly for culinary use or turn them into a lush visual feast to re-create the spirit of the garden indoors. Small pots suffice, but a bountiful herb basket yields larger rewards and a more frequent handful of your favorite spices when you want to perk up a salad or sauce.

Nearly any kind of basket is suitable for an indoor herb garden. A natural fibrous material, such as wicker, combines perfectly in a casual and earthy way, yet is versatile enough for any decor. Metal and wire baskets offer unique shapes, are longer lasting, and can be planted with only a moss liner.

- Direct sun
- Let soil dry out between waterings
- Average room temperature
- Prune regularly; replace plants annually or as needed

The tiered basket that holds this garden is large enough to warrant its own private window and counter space in a large and airy kitchen. The basket not only holds the herbs up to eye level, but it also allows them to drape gracefully over the rims. When a branch of rosemary grows too long, toss it on the grill for a flavor enhancer or crush the leaves for a marinade. Pick off sprigs of thyme and oregano for the pot on the stove or as a garnish for the table. Pay some attention to color and texture as you put together your garden; variegated and crinkly foliage add visual pizzazz as well as flavor.

WHAT YOU'LL NEED

Vigorously growing herbs in 2- to 4-inch pots

Sphagnum moss or moss substitute

Bucket or bowl and spray bottle of water

Heavy plastic

Basket, about 4 inches deep

Peat-based potting mix, moistened

Scissors

Small trowel

Slow-release fertilizer

ONGOING CARE

Water only when the potting mix feels dry to the touch ½ to 1 inch below the surface. Never allow an herb garden to dry out completely, and never overwater. Herbs will die if their roots are soggy. Place basket where herbs will receive at least 6 hours of direct sun a day.

Choose a basket to suit your decorating style and the number of herbs in your garden. It should be large enough to allow ¾ to 1 inch between rootballs and 1 inch underneath after the plants are set in place.

At least 1 hour before you plant, water herbs in their pots and soak the moss in a bucket or bowl of water. Let herbs and moss drain thoroughly.

Ease the plastic liner into the basket so that it fits snugly inside and overlaps the edges. Wait to trim it until you finish planting.

Pour in enough potting mix so that herbs in the center are slightly elevated above those toward the edge. Artfully arrange the tallest plants either in the center or at one side. Set shrubby plants in the middle and those that cascade along the outside.

Loosen the roots of each plant as you position it in the basket. Use scissors to cut through severely bound roots.

Fill spaces between rootballs with potting mix, firming it slightly with your fingers against plant roots as you work. Mist generously to settle the soil; add additional mix, as needed. The finished soil level should be ½ to 1 inch below the basket rim.

Mist foliage and exposed liner to rinse off soil spills. Trim away excess liner, leaving about ½ inch to extend above the soil.

Separate clumps of moistened moss and arrange lightly over the surface, placing strands under herb branchlets and over liner edges. Allow herbs to rest out of direct sun for a day or two.

During the growing season, fertilize with fractional doses each time you water, but expect your herbs to rest in winter; they grow most vigorously from spring through fall.

Dozens of thyme cultivars (center and left) contribute a range of scents, such as lemon, lime, and mint, as well as hearty flavors, including caraway, nutmeg, and nutty pepper. Although any herb collection adds to kitchen decor, it makes sense to pot up the ones you use most often in cooking. Pizza lovers will want to include oregano (right) for its unmistakable, sweet-spicy flavor. Pinch tips frequently, and periodically cut off entire stems at the base to encourage herbs to stay bushy. Set your collection in full sun and try to give it some time outdoors in summer. You may want to have two sets of plants and alternate them between indoors and out.

mediterranean herb plants

◄ Thyme

Wiry branchlets of pungent, red-stemmed 'Lemon Curd' thyme (*Thymus*) drape over a basket rim just begging to be snipped for flavor or garnish. Alternatively, grow this attractive creeper as a ground cover under a sun-loving topiary or a dwarf citrus shrub.

► Rosemary

The neat foliage and cascading habit of pungent rosemary (*Rosmarinus*) suit it perfectly for growing in a tiered basket, though any container will do. In late winter, tiny lilac-blue or white blooms decorate twiggy branches, nearly covering them through early spring. In summer, set plants outdoors in full sun, where they thrive best. Always allow soil to dry out between waterings.

▲ Sage

Purple or red sage (*Salvia officinalis* 'Purpurea', center) is only one of many varieties of garden sage. Other cultivars sport marbled foliage in lovely combinations of gold, cream, green, and lilac, while common sage is pale bluish green (right). During its second year, thyme develops woody stems at the base, but frequent pinching of leaves and stems maintains compact growth. After two years, replace plants.

herb topiaries

Herb topiaries are one of the most versatile forms of all indoor garden plants because they can be placed in any room. Formal arrangements call for matching pairs on a mantelpiece or sideboard, where they draw attention in their own right or direct the eye to a piece of art or a photograph. Standing alone or grouped together, they never fail to dress up a tabletop, but you may want to keep topiaries in the kitchen if the herbs appeal to your culinary instincts.

You can purchase ready-made and actively growing clipped balls or hoops in geometric shapes and animal images, or you can fashion your own. Mediterranean herbs are especially well suited for topiary subjects. They develop strong woody stems and small, densely arranged leaves that welcome clipping — and they reward you with pungent aromas as you work. Good choices are rosemary, myrtle, sweet bay *(Laurus nobilis),* santolina, sage, lavender, and germander *(Teucrium chamaedrys).* An attractive ground cover completes the scene. Here, Irish moss *(Sagina subulata)* softens the hard edge beneath the spiraling stems of a myrtle standard *(Myrtus communis),* while creeping Corsican mint *(Mentha requienii)* unfurls masses of tiny foliage under a dark green rosemary hoop at the right.

- Direct sun
- Let soil dry out between waterings
- Cool temperature
- Long-lived in strong light

If you decide to shape an herb topiary, you'll be practicing patience as much as anything else. It takes time for plants to grow and a willing determination to train them to do what doesn't come naturally.

Woody herb with multiple stems

Wire form for shaping

Container, preferably terra-cotta

Soil-based potting mix

Slow-release fertilizer

Twine ties

Sphagnum moss, moistened, or mat-forming plants

Small clippers or bonsai shears

ONGOING CARE

Place topiary in a warm, sunny location. Water only when soil is dry 1 inch below the surface. As soon as the branchlets remain securely in place, remove ties. From time to time for added enjoyment, move topiary to a tabletop in lower light for use as a decorating accessory.

Some herbs grow faster than others, so make your plant selection based on the amount of time you want to spend snipping and clipping to keep your topiary in shape. Some herbs, such as myrtle and sweet bay, grow quite slowly but are long-lived. Rosemary, santolina, teucrium, and lavender are faster growing.

To train an herb around a hoop, begin with a two-year-old plant with long, multiple stems. (To train a standard, choose an herb with one well-developed stem.)

Select a container that is about equal in height and width to the wire form so that the completed project will have pleasing proportions. (Take the container's horizontal measurement at the rim.) A clay pot is preferred, because it is weightier than plastic and will provide needed stability.

Pot the herb in a fast-draining, soil-based mix with slow-release fertilizer granules added according to package directions. The soil level should be ½ to 1 inch below the rim.

Set wire form as close as possible to the herb's center, pull loose branches snugly over wires, and tie securely in place. Alternatively, wind stems around wires as they grow.

To cover soil and balance overall dimensions, fill the top of the container with moist sphagnum moss or plant a mat-forming species, such as Irish moss (*Sagina subulata*). If you like longer, trailing stems, plant a miniature English ivy (*Hedera helix*), but trim away stems that want to be vertical.

Clip side branches twice a year, once in spring and again in late summer, or as needed to maintain a pleasing shape.

herb topiary plants

▼ **Rosemary**

These plants may be trained as single-stemmed standards or wound around preformed wire shapes in pots of nearly any size. Whereas geraniums (*Pelargonium*) are well adapted to grow as house-plants, rosemary prefers some time outdoors in bright sun-shine. If you do move pots outside, take care that they never dry out completely. In small pots, soil dries fast.

▲ **Geranium**

Scented geraniums (*Pelargonium*) trained on a single stem make wonderful topiaries. You can use them casually to fill a room with the sight and scent of a summer garden, or group them in pairs for a formal arrangement. Lemon, coconut, rose, and nutmeg are but a few of the aromas you'll find. Slow-growing, small-leafed varieties make the choicest topiaries; variegated forms, the most alluring. Begin with a single-stemmed plant 6 to 8 inches tall in a 6- or 8-inch pot. Tie the stem to a slender stake and top it when it reaches 12 inches. With regular and repeated pinching, lower branches will be forced out. Continue clipping them until you arrive at the desired shape.

lavender garden

After centuries of being relegated to soaps and sachets, lavender has gone modern and entered the arena of home decorating, but nothing has replaced its freshness and soothing fragrance in the bath. Here is where you'll use it most — foliage and flower, fresh or dried, crushed to release essential oil or left intact to float around you. Lavender's restorative qualities not only soothe the body but also perfume cupboards and closets or any indoor space where air is stale. Hang bundled dried stems wherever you want their invigorating aroma, or arrange them as you would fresh flowers.

Flaglike bracts of Spanish lavender (*Lavandula stoechas*, right) are as colorful as they are aromatic. Dwarf forms of English lavender (*L. angustifolia*, lower left) may also be grown in containers.

Like other woody-stemmed herbs, lavender must have 6 hours of light a day during active growth to flourish. A south-facing window is excellent, but better yet is a period outdoors after you've harvested the flowers and stems. For an uninterrupted lavender display, keep two sets of plants growing and alternate them indoors and out. After flowering, cut back plants halfway, give them a soaking, and set them outside in full sun. When new buds begin to open, bring the plants indoors.

After the second bloom, repot the plants to allow for the next year's growth. To ensure vigor and good foliage color, use either slow-release granules in the potting mix or a diluted fertilizer solution with each watering. Always provide good drainage, never allow soil to dry out completely, and cut back on watering in winter.

- Direct sun
- Let soil dry out between waterings
- Average room temperature
- Plants live three years or longer

glassed-in gardens

Glass protection for growing plants is nothing new, but its interpretation takes on a whole new dimension every few decades. You may never wish to top the Victorian craze for building fanciful glass cases or elaborate conservatories, but you will love the ethereal combination of glass and plants that evolved during ages past. Glass goes well beyond beauty in its appeal to the gardener by serving the very practical purpose of preserving not only humidity and moisture while admitting light but also our ambitions in growing an indoor garden.

bell jar garden

Few indoor gardens brighten a winter's day like a garden under glass. Just the opposite of a snowy scene inside a glass globe, a garden under the protection of a glistening cloche transports us to warmer climes where tropical sunshine reigns.

The most beautiful protective domes are clear, glimmering glass, though some are plastic and many are tinted green. While a crystal bell jar may win the beauty prize, an inverted glass bowl serves just as well. The glass's purpose is to maintain a hospitable environment by admitting light and retaining moisture.

In this garden, clear glass domes rest on glass supports to hover cleverly above bird's-nest ferns (*Asplenium*) and miniature flamingo flower (*Anthurium*), holding in warmth and moisture while allowing free movement of air.

Dwarf and slow-growing plants work best under a glass cover. Here is the place for a hard-to-grow species – perhaps a rare begonia, a miniature gloxinia (*Sinningia*), a 'Starsprite' *Centradenia*, or an African violet (*Saint paulia*) – that thrives on an uninterrupted supply of warm, moist air.

As good a portable mini greenhouse as it is, a bell jar comes with a warning or two. Too much moisture can be as fatal to your plants as too little, and fresh air is as essential as water. You can waylay any problems that may occur by resting the glass dome on a stable support 1 or 2 inches above the table or countertop or by simply removing it for a brief period every day.

- Bright, indirect light
- Keep soil lightly moist
- Average room temperature
- Long-lived with routine care

wardian case garden

Like many valuable discoveries, the garden-in-a-bottle idea happened quite by chance. In 1829, Dr. Nathaniel Ward was pursuing one of his scientific inquiries in the smoky air of London when he noticed sprouts growing in a corked bottle where he had placed the chrysalis of a moth. Warmed by the sun, moisture from the garden soil in the bottle condensed and dripped down inside the glass, making it possible for some errant plant seeds to germinate and grow. He quickly built cases to house ferns and other plants that never prospered for him outdoors. Here, indeed, was a new way to make a garden.

When Ward's success was revealed, avid Victorian gardeners hastened to coddle tropical plants in their homes — a passion that continues today around the world. We no longer build large wooden cases to house indoor gardens, but we do still enjoy the tropical plants that Ward's discovery made possible for botanists and collectors to ship home through cold, salty sea air. Those species retrieved

- Bright, indirect light
- Constant moisture
- Average room temperature
- Replace overcrowded plants

from faraway habitats have given rise to our modern favorites. Here, a ruffled African violet, a delicate maidenhair fern, and Irish moss nestle inside this modern interpretation of the Wardian case.

You can be as creative as Dr. Ward in selecting a case for your indoor garden. Look beyond glass boxes dedicated to plant growing and consider lanterns, hurricanes intended for candles, and any other waterproof enclosure.

WHAT YOU'LL NEED

Moisture-loving tropical or woodland plants

Waterproof container with removable top

Peat-based soil mix, moistened

Slow-release fertilizer

Garden trowel

Rainwater or distilled water

Spray bottle

Small clippers or bonsai shears

ONGOING CARE

Water only when potting mix feels dry to the touch just beneath the surface. Lift lid or other opening for several hours every day or two to circulate air. If spots of mold or mildew appear, remove lid for two or three days to increase air circulation and rid infection. Keep glass clean and the case away from direct sun.

Like the Victorians, you can adapt an antique wooden case to house a tabletop garden. If you decide to go that route, be sure to seal and waterproof the interior. You might also consider fitting it with mirrors on three sides to intensify light, which would broaden your options of where to place it in a room. With or without mirrors, a fluorescent light fixed on the interior ceiling and controlled by a timer provides light on dim days; a small fan circulates air.

Double-check the container to make sure it is watertight before filling it with potting mix. Purchase a sterile, peat-based product to avoid introducing any pathogens into the closed environment. A 2- to 4-inch depth is ideal.

Add a few granules of slow-release fertilizer at planting time and replace them according to package directions. If you opt for a liquid fertilizer, apply only half doses monthly from early spring through early fall, and allow plants to rest during winter.

Where there is no drainage, moisten soil mix slowly as you plant to avoid saturation but ensure that roots can access moisture. Use only tepid rainwater or distilled water to avoid chemical buildup that can shock and damage plants.

Firm soil gently around plant roots and lightly mist soil to settle it. Mist fern and moss foliage, but take care to avoid wetting African violet leaves.

As plants grow, clip off wandering stems that threaten to cover neighboring foliage or block light. Pinch off faded violet blossoms for extended flowering.

Many other plants will grow in a Wardian case. Whatever your selection, if you plant several different ones, check each plant's cultural requirements so that all will flourish in similar conditions.

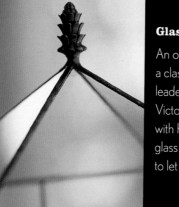

Glass Details

An opulent collection takes on a classic air when displayed in a leaded-glass case reminiscent of Victorian designs. Look for cases with hinged lids and removable glass panels that can be opened to let in a breath of fresh air.

◄ Maidenhair fern

The thin, delicate foliage of maidenhair fern (*Adiantum*) contrasts sharply with its dark, wiry stems. Apple green leaflets seem to float fanlike in broken, triangular patterns along the length of each frond. When stems outgrow their space, snip them off at the base.

wardian case plants

▲ African violet

Fancy ruffled blossoms with perky yellow centers distinguish the African violet (*Saint paulia*) as a focal point in this encased garden. Average room temperature – a little warmer during the day, a little cooler at night – high humidity, regular fertilizer doses, and even moisture will keep it blooming for months. Keep the plant away from direct sunlight, and turn it every week to maintain balanced growth. As old leaves die, gently pull them away from the main stem. In a smaller garden, opt for a semi-miniature, miniature, or micro-miniature cultivar; be sure to reduce the scale of companion plants as well.

► Irish moss

The slender leaves of Irish moss (*Sagina subulata*) are similar to those of woodland mosses; they cover the soil and provide a cushiony base for an encased garden. Trim stems that want to grow over the edges and thin out those in the center that mound up unattractively.

terrarium garden

The first terrariums traveled the high seas for weeks if not months on end, preserving exotic flora from faraway tropical places for European plant collectors and conservators. You can cherish your own private plant collections under modern decorator glass and promote a humid atmosphere in which they can flourish.

The terrarium container establishes the mood of your garden, no matter which plants you choose. Thick glass is a reminder of the 1960s and '70s, when a houseplant revival led to an explosion of interest in bottle gardens. Thin crystalline containers are more suited to a contemporary decor, while leaded-glass boxes come in many styles and are welcome just about anywhere.

There is no shortage of plants and plant combinations from which to choose, but what you don't want in a terrarium is as important as what you do want. You don't want rampant growth or tall spindly stems that call for constant pinching. You may not want a flowering plant that drops its petals after flowering or holds them until they're snipped off. You do want compatibility in a self-contained ecosystem so you don't have to fuss over the garden or replace plants frequently. And you do want something out of the ordinary that makes the entire project satisfying, worthy of admiration, and uniquely your own. In the example at left, pale green and gold reverberate between primroses and Scotch moss, a perfect pair for their color echoes and similar cultural needs.

- Bright, indirect light
- Even moisture
- High humidity
- Average room temperature
- Varied life spans

Small plants in 6-packs or 2-inch containers

Horticultural charcoal

Clean, clear glass container, preferably with an opening large enough to admit your hand

Pea or aquarium gravel, rinsed (optional)

Sterile, soil-based potting mix

Scissors

Long-handled spoon

Spray bottle

Distilled water

Sphagnum moss mulch (optional)

Ornamental accessories (optional)

ONGOING CARE

Water only when soil feels dry to the touch; fertilize sparingly. Replace plants that droop or develop spindly stems; correct moisture and light levels to avoid future problems. Remove spent blossoms on flowering plants and any leaves that drop off.

Experiment with several plant combinations to arrive at the look you want. Base your selections on foliage texture and color, growth rate, plant compatibility, and the presence or absence of flowers.

Pour a ½-inch layer of charcoal chips evenly over the bottom of container and cover with another ½-inch layer of pea or aquarium gravel, if desired, to help aerate roots. Add several inches of slightly moistened potting soil.

Rose Garden

Any size bottle or jar becomes a terrarium once soil and plants go inside. Protect a miniature tea rose overnight by stoppering the top, then open the jar during the day for good air circulation.

Remove most of the soil from nursery plants and trim away any coiled or wrapped roots. Use a long-handled spoon to set smaller plants around the outside and taller specimens in the center.

Spray the inside of the glass to wash away spills, then mist foliage and soil to settle plants. Use utmost care in judging how much water to spray into the garden, because soil should be moist, not saturated. A damp sponge may be all you need to clean off the inside of the glass.

If no creeping plant covers the soil, lay thin clumps of shredded sphagnum moss over the surface and mist again. Arrange ornamental accessories for decoration, if desired.

Place terrarium away from direct sunlight to avoid overheating air and plants inside.

◄ Scotch moss

Golden green Scotch moss (*Sagina subulata* 'Aurea') masses mosslike over the soil, retaining moisture. It appreciates the same humid, mildly fertile environment as its plush vine and primrose companions.

► Primrose

The compact tufts of apple green foliage on this primrose (*Primula* 'Mahogany Sunrise') fit neatly into terrarium jars, where flowers are borne to perfection. Fine gold tracery outlines deep mahogany red single flowers with large golden yellow eyes. Frequent but very light doses of a balanced fertilizer paired with a humid atmosphere result in nearly nonstop bloom. Situate this primrose garden in very bright light but out of direct sun.

▼ Plush vine

Bronzy purple plush vine (*Mikania dentata* 'Purple Haze') from tropical woodlands basks contentedly under glassed-in humidity. Deeply lobed foliage bristles softly under bright, indirect light and covers the soil with trailing stems. Shorten them frequently to maintain control; fertilize lightly each month.

terrarium plants

foliage gardens

There is no denying the universal appeal of green in the garden. In all its varied shades and hues, green rests the eye, fills in space, adds dimension, and balances form. But for radiant dynamism, look beyond green and opt instead for creamy variegation, hot pink or orange, and vivid – even shocking – tints from around the color wheel. The foliage of many species comes alive with color, outshining flowers here and there and lasting for a very long time.

As you select foliage plants for your indoor garden, pay attention to leaf shape and texture. Wrinkles and creases etched in contrasting hues stand out in strong patterns worthy of a prominent place on a tabletop. Here, a rex begonia assumes a painterly pose as morning light flows through its translucent stems and leaves.

ivy tower

Preformed wire frames weren't invented for the busy gardener, but they shave years off training foliage plants into whimsical shapes to suit your fancy. Turning away from slow-growing shrubby plants speeds the process even more when a fast-growing vine, such as English ivy *(Hedera helix)*, races to the finish within a season or two.

Training an ivy topiary may seem like a serious endeavor, but it should be taken lightly. Once a bunny or a bear is covered in green, you have no choice but to smile, so you may as well do the same with a cone, a globe, an obelisk, or a wreath. And green isn't the only option. There are hundreds of ivy cultivars from which you can choose chartreuse, bluish, or purplish black tints, as well as variegations in cream, white, yellow, and gold.

- Bright, indirect light
- Allow soil surface to dry before watering
- Cool temperature
- Long-lived

Very large wire forms call for multiple plants set around a pot. Their dangling stems can be lifted, tied, and trimmed for a fast cover in all directions. Smaller wires need only one or two plants, or you'll end up with more stems than you can handle. For a more free-form design, allow some of the stems to cascade over the side.

WHAT YOU'LL NEED

3 young ivy plants with several trailing stems

Granular, slow-release fertilizer

Soil-based potting mix

6- to 8-inch clay pot

Garden trowel

Spiral tower form

Plant ties

Scissors or pruning shears

ONGOING CARE

Place ivy tower in a bright but cool site out of direct sun. Water only when soil feels dry on the surface. Remove ties as soon as stems remain securely in place. Continue to train new growth onto the tower until foliage is crowded, then prune stems to maintain a pleasing shape.

Not all varieties of English ivy are speedy growers, so you'll want to check before you buy to make sure they have the characteristics you're looking for. In fact, some cultivars grow quite slowly and should be avoided altogether when you want long lengths. Select a clay pot, which provides weight and the stability needed to prevent the tower from becoming top heavy.

Following package directions, mix granular, slow-release fertilizer into soil-based potting mix. Fill the pot to within 1 inch of the top.

Plant small ivies at equal distances around the perimeter of the container.

Wedge the tower form deep into the pot, completely vertical and secure. Wind the longest stems of each plant onto wires, leaving one or two on the outside of each plant to trail. Tie stems as needed to hold them in place.

Prune any unruly stems and thin occasionally over time to avoid a crowded, unkempt appearance.

Ivy is amazingly adaptable and able to thrive in dim interiors, but if long stem sections develop between leaves, move the container into brighter light. Always avoid direct sun, which burns foliage. Ivy grows fastest in strong but indirect light.

Ivy Standard

Twist or braid stems around a thin, vertical post before training ivy over a globe. Choose small-leafed ivies for pots 4 inches wide or smaller.

Ivy Variegation

Light shining on ivy's pale variegation casts a dappled iridescence over the foliage. How each variety responds depends on which pigments are present or absent. Pale ribbons of white or cream along the margins highlight leaf shapes.

Marbling and solid blocks in leaf centers give the appearance of a floral presence strewn throughout the foliage. Irregular speckles scattered over leaf surfaces reflect points of light, even when out of direct sun.

Given the enormous diversity of leaf shapes and sizes, you may want to choose two varieties — two variegated or one variegated and one plain — and entwine them as they grow for a happy marriage of form and function. Each type differs in detail and delicacy and never grows boring.

ivy window trim

Ivy is so amenable to training that it's tempting to let it go on forever. A window, doorway, or mirror frame outlined in leafy green is a good subject for an inveterate ivy lover. Long vines need not be trimmed at all, merely supported and allowed to drape in swags or long, trailing streamers. Over this north-facing window, ivy blurs the line between indoors and out, seemingly transporting the room-side garden into open air. To exaggerate the feeling, allow vines to cascade repeatedly like a living curtain. Translucent variegated varieties admit light, yet screen casements for a bit of privacy. Before choosing just one variety, consider combining the leaf colors and shapes of different ones.

Upward mobility makes sense with plants when indoor space is at a premium, but you'll need to levy some controls on ivy's tenacious and runaway habits. In front of a window, it's best to guide it away from painted molding and onto chain links (shown at left), a stout cord, or another support that will boost it to great heights.

When too many stems leave you wondering how to use them, clip off a few and trail them down a table for a festive centerpiece. Cut stems last for days out of water.

To soften the severity of hard lines in post-and-beam interiors, try placing pots around structural supports and letting ivy climb, as long as leafy stems don't grow completely out of reach. If you allow ivy to support itself on posts with clinging aerial rootlets, you may need to provide transparent nylon fishing line to get it started.

Spacious interiors also allow for other unusual ivy displays. Trained on a simple trellis, ivy will grow onto a screen of nearly any size and serve

- Bright, indirect light
- Even moisture
- Average room temperature
- Long-lived

as a room divider or living sculpture against a bare wall. On a tabletop, a cascading form will completely transform a simple, worn surface.

variegated-foliage garden

In a controlled color scheme where garden and furniture mingle, variegated plants play a critical role. Relying on the optical effect of echoed foliage highlights, you can match containers, fabric, and other accessories to leaf variegation or, conversely, show them in sharp contrast.

Here, pale, wide-spreading veins of Kris plant (*Alocasia sanderiana*) cut through the metallic sheen of its wavy black-green foliage, creating a singular, dramatic effect when set against a plain background. Bold, exaggerated heart-shaped leaves seem to float at the tips of thin, arching stems.

Such a minimalist foliage garden deserves a high profile in any interior. Try placing it where backlighting will emphasize the pale venation and where there is no pattern to compete with its delicately sculpted outlines. Set against richly colored walls or painted furniture and facing little competition, Kris plant becomes one with its setting and provides a bold finishing touch to contemporary furnishings and stark color schemes.

Introducing a vibrant foliage garden into any room never fails to energize a tired decor. Try massing thick, multicolored croton (*Codiaeum variegatum* var. *pictum*) foliage in bright light against wood paneling to relieve a ponderous atmosphere, or set plants where bright yellow shouts out for a daring companion. Dress up undersized tabletops with variegated tufts of Lilliputian Peperomia and Fittonia or a simple sprig of coleus (*Solenostemon*) rooting in a glass of water.

- **Bright, filtered light**
- **Slightly moist soil**
- **Warm room temperature**
- **Long-lived with regular care**

Use variegated foliage, also, to enliven monotone plant groups in miniature dish gardens as well as among an assembly of pots. In a single container of compatible plants – those with the same hue and cultural needs – limit variegation to one species but mix several plants with colorful stripes and splotches into a collection in individual containers.

◄ 'Iron Cross' begonia

Glistening hairs cover the stems of this 'Iron Cross' begonia, lifting its distinctive leaf pattern, which has made it a favorite among thousands of hybrids. High humidity, consistent moisture, and bright light out of direct sun sustain healthy foliage. Provide a humidity tray or mist frequently in dry indoor air.

► Painted-leaf rex begonia

Tried-and-true houseplants, rex begonias, such as this spectacular painted-leaf hybrid, enter a new age when they become one with their surroundings. Here, explosive hot color resonates between foliage highlights, container, and plant stand. Some varieties display kaleidoscopic leaf patterns in shades of pink, green, yellow, gray, and red or have bright undersides in shocking hues.

flower gardens

There's no doubt that flowers fresh from the garden are also fresh from the heart, but the garden need not be in the backyard or behind a picket fence. It could be blooming to perfection right in your living room. Your choice of blossoming stems is limited, of course, when the garden grows indoors, but a range of options still lets you reflect your style and taste. Needless to say, a tabletop garden won't be massive, yet a single, understated bloom that radiates its charm on a gray day lifts the spirits and enlivens any room. With few rivals of its exquisite beauty, this dendrobium orchid seems to float on pale, gossamer wings.

basket of orchids

Thousands of orchids beg to sprawl through tree branches in steaming jungles, but a good number can live happily indoors and be exquisitely displayed on table-tops. Fluttering moth orchids *(Phalaenopsis)* are among the easiest to grow, but oncidiums, lady-slippers *(Paphiopedilum),* and miniature cymbidiums also do well. Their picture-perfect, elegant blooms can often be cajoled into reappearing for a second show with just a little extra care and attention.

Orchids are most at home in a warm, humid environment. A dedicated garden room that can handle excess moisture is ideal, but any well-lit spot harboring a nearby tray of water satisfies their basic needs. You may want to grow an orchid garden under fluorescent lights and move it into a place of prominence when the blossoms are in their prime. This mesh basket chock-full of oncidiums is ideally placed out of direct sun but in bright, filtered light. Just remember that the right light and humidity are the real keys to success and the forerunners to many months of flowering.

- Bright, indirect light
- Allow soil to dry between waterings
- High humidity
- Warm days, cool nights
- Long-lived with regular care

If you've never grown orchids before, don't be put off by fears of failure. Stick with one of the more common varieties and get to know it. Start with a plant in riveting blossom so you'll know what to look for when flowering time comes around again. Don't ignore the foliage, though. That's what you'll be seeing and feeding for more than half the year, while the plant readies itself for another season of bloom.

WHAT YOU'LL NEED

Orchids with healthy roots and foliage

Rustproof metal basket with adequate drainage

Fibrous sphagnum moss, tree fern fiber, or coconut fiber

Horticultural charcoal

Medium-sized fir bark orchid potting mix

Hand trowel

Containers with drainage holes (optional)

Thin bamboo plant stakes

Pruning shears

Rainwater or distilled water

Fertilizer formulated for orchids

ONGOING CARE

In warm conditions, water once or twice a week with rainwater or distilled water; treated water can be fatal. Apply an orchid fertilizer according to package directions or use a weak solution with each watering. Maintain constant humidity, particularly during winter, with a humidifier or a pebble-filled tray of water under the pot, or mist frequently. Repot when planting medium breaks down and compacts.

There are two ways to construct an orchid garden in a basket. One is to sink a group of plants in their pots and surround them with moss or coconut fiber. The other method is to plant directly in the basket, though you will need a waterproof area in which to work so the basket can drain after watering.

Line a decorative metal basket with well-moistened moss, tree fern fiber, or coconut fiber. Keep layers loose but thick enough to prevent bark from slipping through.

Combine a handful of charcoal with orchid potting mix; pour a mound several inches deep on top of the moss.

Using a trowel, set long rhizomes 1 inch below the rim, with the oldest part of the stems toward the outside. Set orchids with individual stems nearer the center, with the base of the lowest leaves about 1 inch below the rim. (When sinking pots, rest them on moss so their tops are 1 inch below the basket rim.)

Working from the outside to the center, fill in with bark potting mix, firming it around roots as you would potting soil. Stake plants upright, if necessary. Cover the surface with moss. Water freely and drain well.

One of the best ways to become familiar with your orchid's water needs is to lift the basket from time to time. Immediately after watering, it feels heavy; when dry it feels light. The trick is to identify the weight at an in-between point to avoid over- and under-watering.

As bark potting mix decomposes and compacts, it must be refreshed to prevent roots from rotting. Repot orchids every other year after they have bloomed, during a period of dormancy before new growth begins. Cut away brown, dead roots, shorten healthy ones as needed, and firm new bark chips snugly over them.

Orchid Pots

Clay pots with honeycombed or pierced sides drain fast and allow ample air circulation, critical factors in preventing root rot and engendering long life among all orchid species.

basket of orchids

◄ Cymbidium orchid

These orchids go to great lengths to impress us with their cheery winter blooms. Standard hybrids, which thrive in very cool nighttime temperatures, often soar 3 to 4 feet high, laden with 4-inch blooms. Fortunately, less-demanding miniatures are only 1½ to 2 feet tall, and they fit more readily on a tabletop and thrive in warmth. These charmers begin to flower in November, just in time to dispel winter gloom and add to holiday decor. Individual flowers, which come in nearly every color, are smaller than the standards, but three to four dozen may appear on each spike amid grasslike leaves. Dwarf species are highly aromatic and more slender in flower and foliage.

► Dendrobium orchid

Regal sprays flow from dendrobium orchids in reward for special care. More sensitive overall than some other species but possessing the same inherent grace and lavish beauty, they are no more demanding in their basic call for humidity and bright, filtered light. Where they differ is in individual needs. Inquire when you purchase a dendrobium whether it is a deciduous, cool-growing species that wants a long winter rest with little or no water or an evergreen, warmgrowing species that needs moisture throughout the year.

orchid under glass

To an orchid, spending time in a mini indoor greenhouse is the equivalent of our lounging in a spa. You can accommodate an orchid by setting pots of small and dwarf species in a deep glass vase or bowl that admits bright light and holds in humidity, both of which foster vigor. Because it's difficult to remove excess water from deep vases, rest orchid pots on a layer of polished stones to hold them above the water after the pots drain. Or use a kitchen baster to siphon off potentially disastrous standing pools.

Delicate miniature blossoms of *Phalaenopsis* (left), *Oncidium* (center), and lady-slipper (*Paphiopedilum*, right) crown low clusters of leaves in a glassed-in, humid-rich environment.

Set such a collection in bright, filtered light but out of direct sun, which will burn foliage. Always expose orchids to free air circulation, especially those you set under a glass cloche. Take advantage of this apparent air of opulence by featuring your glassed-in collection prominently anywhere in the house. After a week or so, move orchids back to bright light.

As with most other plants, maintaining a balance of conditions ensures a healthy orchid. Glass helps protect orchids from drafts near windows and heat registers, but too much enclosure reduces a supply of fresh air.

Similarly, glass helps preserve humidity, but too much moisture on roots, leaves, and flowers promotes bacterial and fungal infections. By inspecting your orchid every few days, you will avoid extremes and enjoy many years of beauty.

- Bright, indirect light
- Allow to dry between waterings
- Warm days, cool nights
- Long-lived with regular care

Moth orchids

The moth orchid (*Phalaenopsis*), so called for its fluttering habit on long, arching stems, is favored for its longevity and easy care. It thrives in average household conditions that are cooler at night – 60 to 65°F – than during the day. A drop to 55°F at night for several weeks in autumn is ideal to promote bloom. Whitish green aerial roots often grow out of the potting mix, extending several inches over the surface and often down the sides, signaling vigor and proper care. Keep an eye on the thick foliage. It demands high humidity, but overwatering turns leaves yellow. To encourage repeat bloom after a first flowering, cut the stem just below the point where the first flower appeared.

Oncidium orchids

Of the hundreds of oncidium orchids, each is more scintillating than the last. Delicate yellow and brownish red, white, or pink blossoms on branching sprays imitate dancing dolls, one species' common name. If you grow your orchid garden under fluorescent lights, you may want to put only the blooms on display. Cut stems last for weeks and blend well in flower arrangements with other long-stemmed beauties, such as delphinium, lilies, and phlox.

orchids under glass

bromeliad garden

Stunning bromeliads planted on a moss-covered log or individually in pots could easily illustrate a theme of tropical splendor. Brilliantly hued blossoms and floral bracts vary wildly from genus to genus and species to species, rivaling spectacular foliar patterns and shapes and looking very much like exotic plumage riveted in place. As a group, bromeliads have the unusual feature of being able to absorb moisture and nourishment through pores in their leaves.

Bromeliads are often referred to as air plants, because most develop few or no anchoring roots. Instead, many live as epiphytes by clinging to rocks or hanging in trees; bluish-leafed *Aechmea* and dangling, bejeweled queen's tears *(Billbergia)* are two such examples. Others, including stemless *Cryptanthus* and spiky *Dyckia,* are terrestrial. Spidery-looking *Tillandsia,* wider-spreading *Guzmania* and *Neoregelia,* and many others grow in or out of soil.

- Bright, filtered light
- Rainwater or distilled water in cupped rosettes
- Average room temperature
- Varied life spans

Some bromeliads flower only after living for many years as foliage plants. Those that do bloom at a relatively young age hold flowers only briefly, but their showier bracts create a center of attention for weeks or months, after which time the foliage, except that of *Dyckia,* withers and dies. However, young offsets continue on to produce new plants. Many rosette-forming species have a cuplike center that must be kept filled with water. New foliage spills around it in a dazzling display, looking convincingly like an inflorescence but often lined with minute scales and prickly spines.

WHAT YOU'LL NEED

Small bromeliad rosettes

Sphagnum moss

Bowl or bucket

Rainwater or distilled water

Branch or driftwood, washed and rinsed

Florist's wire

Cork bark

Spray bottle

Water-soluble fertilizer

ONGOING CARE

Maintain a constant supply of water in cuplike rosette centers, but change it from time to time by inverting plants and refilling. Mist foliage several times a week. Dissolve fractional doses of a complete, all-purpose fertilizer in water and spray monthly, except in winter.

Once you're hooked on epiphytes, you'll want to move from a simple bromeliad log displaying a single species to a more complex epiphyte branch with forks and cavities where a multiplicity of species can nestle in flamboyant style.

Before you begin, soak sphagnum moss in water for up to 1 hour, then drain thoroughly.

Wrap moss around base of bromeliads, enclosing any roots that are present. Moss clumps should be at least as large as your fist.

Nutrient Sprays

With few roots to absorb nutrients, bromeliads rely on monthly water-soluble fertilizer sprays to nourish their foliage. Use drops of a product formulated for African violets or fractional doses of a general-purpose fertilizer.

For ease in handling, temporarily affix a bromeliad and moss clump to a branch with a small single wire twisted closed.

To hold plant firmly in place and prevent the wire from cutting roots and foliage, place a small slab of cork bark over the top of the moss-covered base and wrap wire around several times. To hide the wire, run it over several strands or small clumps of moss as you work.

Gently wedge the moss-encased plants into carved-out depressions and natural hollows, letting your imagination lead you deep into a rain-forest scene.

Fasten all plants securely in place. Periodically, douse bromeliad garden in water to simulate a refreshing rainstorm. Mist daily and never fail to keep rosette cups full.

Alternatively, plant epiphytes in a loose, fast-draining potting mix containing no limestone. Allow pots to become half dry before rewatering, but mist foliage daily.

bromeliad garden plants

◄ Tillandsia

The many *Tillandsia* species vary from lichenlike Spanish moss to narrow leafy forms with brightly colored, overlapping floral bracts that last for weeks. After bloom, each leafy rosette slowly dies and is replaced by offsets produced by the parent plant. Those with bulbous bases should be misted but not soaked. Other types may be soaked for up to 1 hour.

► Bromeliads

Bromeliads, such as this *Tillandsia*, live on rough surfaces of rock and tree bark in tropical environments. Indoors, thin stone slabs and chunks of tree branches provide a realistic substitute. Always place a bromeliad garden in bright, indirect light and provide high humidity and excellent air circulation. A fertilizer low in nitrogen is best.

flowering shrubs and vines

Gardeners dream of strolling through an orchard, pausing under a vine-covered arbor, plucking fresh fruit and enjoying it on the spot. The dream can be reality even indoors when tender fruits are part of the garden plan and a flowering vine is trained on a support. Not all woody-stemmed plants thrive indoors, but many do, as long as they consistently receive 4 to 6 hours of direct sun a day, year-round.

Looking very much like a miniature orange tree, this shrubby kumquat (*Fortunella*) turns winter into spring with a bountiful crop of delicious fruits. Other shrubs, such as abutilon, citrus, brunfelsia, camellia, hibiscus, fuchsia, and hydrangea, may also be grown.

Bougainvillea, passionflower (*Passiflora*), mandevilla, pink jasmine (*Jasminum polyanthum*), and star jasmine (*Trachelospermum jasminoides*) are vines that grow quite successfully indoors. Where space allows, leave them to stretch their stems on a support or, alternatively, clip them regularly into a bushy shape or train them bonsai-fashion.

Several weeks of outdoor air and sunshine in summer help keep shrubs and vines vigorous, but the transition going either indoors or out must be gradual, because a sudden change in environment may cause leaves to drop. Plan to give your plant a week or two in semishade to ease each move.

Planted in small pots (2-gallon size or smaller) and pruned to shape, both shrubs and vines are transformed into treasures for display on a tabletop, where their valued flowers set a room aglow.

- Direct sun
- Evenly moist soil
- Average room temperature, cooler in winter
- Long-lived

◀ Meyer lemon

The fruits of Meyer lemon (*Citrus meyeri*) differ from classic lemons in being smaller, smoother, thinner skinned, juicier, more acidic, and clearer orange in color. The great benefit of growing a Meyer variety comes from year-round flowering and fruits that are borne even on very young trees. The size of the container you use determines the plant's ultimate size. Plants in a 6- to 8-inch pot can be kept under 2 feet tall for many years. Give your tree at least 4 hours of direct sun a day and as much time outdoors as possible during the summer. Shorten branches by half when they appear leggy. Keep the soil moist, and feed plants twice monthly with a balanced product.

shrubs and vines

▶ Kumquat

It seems that kumquat *(Fortunella)* makes up in performance what it lacks in name. White flowers with an orange-blossom scent decorate the tree in spring and summer and are followed by heavy crops of tiny, sweet and tangy fruits that ripen slowly, ready to eat in fall or winter with no peeling required. Unlikely to grow beyond 3 feet in a pot, kumquat insists on its own space in direct sun. Some types bear spines on their stems and branches and aren't as user-friendly as those without. Smaller varieties are citrus hybrids; orangequat is sweeter and limequat makes a good lime substitute.

◀ Bougainvillea

In cold-winter climates, tender vines, such as bougainvillea, grow only as annuals unless they're brought inside as soon as the thermometer heads toward freezing. Once in warmer quarters, they continue to call for at least 4 hours of bright sun a day. However, don't expect them to bloom profusely, as they do in summer, because they require a rest period during the darkest days, when they're likely to drop their leaves. As soon as growth begins in late winter, cut back long, wispy stems by one third to one half and resume normal care of watering and fertilizing as buds break open. Leaf loss during other seasons indicates stress from over- or under-watering or inadequate exposure to light.

seasonal gardens

As each season lingers and we anticipate the next, it's time to plan ahead, gather new plants, and rearrange the garden – even if it's in the compact space of a tabletop. What's more natural, after all, than planting a garden to celebrate the onset of a new season? Spring is the most dynamic time of year, as bulbs and grasses rise again. During busy summer and autumn days, it's easy to rely on old favorites right out of a cottage garden. In winter, gardening may end beyond the windowsill, but not all plants are ready for a rest. Indoors, the spirit of the garden continues, not just in clipped boughs and cuttings taking root in a vase but also in a vibrant array of captivating evergreens.

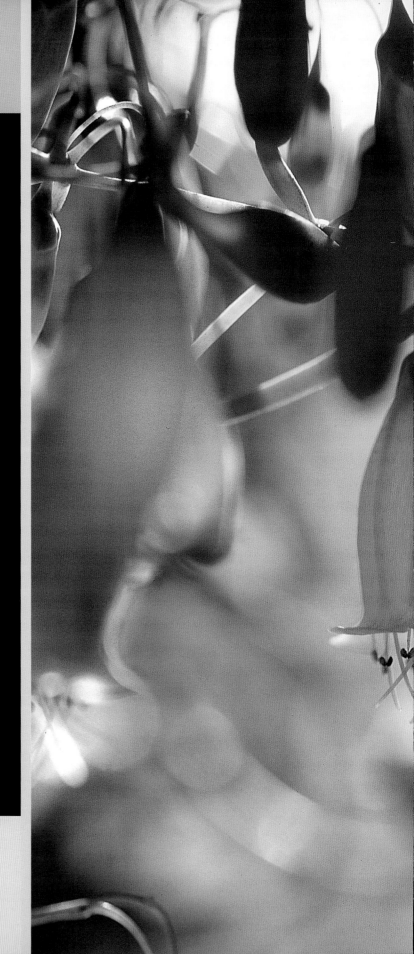

early-spring garden

If a basketful of posies sounds like spring, looks like spring, and smells like spring — it must be springtime in the garden. Just the sight of a primrose-filled basket inspires a gardener to get out the potting soil and start digging once again.

Of the many types of primroses (*Primula*), those in the Polyanthus group are most suited to growing indoors. Their classic petals marked with bright yellow centers cluster atop short stems in striking contrast to low rosettes of crinkled, grass-green foliage.

Miniature hybrids, shown at left, take on a low profile perfect for a tabletop garden. Taller types may have larger blossoms and floppier stems that bend under their weight, but all primroses flaunt flamboyant colors as they herald the end of winter and set the stage for a long show of spring blooms.

Nearly any low basket will hold such a garden. It should be sturdy and woven tightly enough to conceal the inner liner. You'll need a sheet of heavy black plastic fitted into the bottom and overlapping the sides before covering the base with a premoistened, sterilized, soilless potting mix.

Have on hand enough primroses in 4-inch pots that, when set shoulder to shoulder, will completely fill the bottom of the basket. Work just a little potting mix between plants as you set each one, pushing them together so foliage covers the surface.

Water very lightly, keeping in mind that there is no drainage in the basket and that standing water will cause yellowing of leaves and a fast demise of the garden.

- Bright, indirect light
- Evenly moist soil
- Cool temperature
- Discard after bloom

Trim the plastic liner so that it remains hidden ½ inch below the inside rim, and arrange foliage to spill over the edge. To prolong the bloom period, snip off individual flowers as they fade until the last one remains in the cluster. Then remove the stout stem at the base.

grass garden

Few gardens are more understated than one of plain grass, yet such a planting is imbued with richness as it beckons the senses to touch fine soft blades, observe high gloss, and smell freshness. An indoor grass garden plays on the memory, too, calling up the scent of newly mown grass and images of childhood play on sweeping lawns. For the urban dweller, it's a link with the countryside; for those in suburbia, it's a pleasant patch of green that never makes demands on the lawn mower.

Indoors, slender young fields of green, green annual ryegrass *(Lolium multiflorum)* announce from a mantelpiece that spring has arrived. Grass can also extend from a homey touch in a bright kitchen window to a dining room table, where candles and silver make it as elegant as you wish. It becomes a stylistic accessory to set in front of a mirror, decorate a mantelpiece, or pair with an objet d'art. But unlike many other tabletop gardens, a garden of grass has its

- Direct sun or bright light
- Even moisture
- Average room temperature
- Lives for months

whimsical side, too. You can use it playfully in an Easter basket with colored eggs, have it growing out the top of a clay figurine, or plant it wherever your imagination wants it to go. It won't last forever, but you can re-create it again in nearly no time at all.

WHAT YOU'LL NEED

Annual ryegrass seed

Planting tray with drainage holes

Soil-based potting mix

Slow-release granular fertilizer

Garden trowel

Spray bottle of water

Plastic wrap

Long-bladed scissors

ONGOING CARE

Check soil daily for moisture. Water as soon as the surface is dry to the touch—it dries out rapidly when indoor humidity is low. Trim blades every few days during fast growth to encourage density. Turn containers once or twice a week to expose all sides to light and prevent grass from leaning in one direction.

This is one garden that grows from start to finish under the deft hand and watchful eye of a gardener. Plan ahead a bit — about four to six weeks — to jump-start your project so the garden is up and growing before it goes on display. Annual ryegrass seed germinates in days, but it takes several weeks for the carpet to thicken.

In a 2- or 3-inch-deep seed tray, sow fresh seed thickly over warm, moist soil mixed with slow-release fertilizer, covering the surface completely. Top with a very thin layer of soil. Mist heavily with warm water, let drain, and cover lightly with clear plastic, allowing some air circulation.

Wheat Grass

Vivid green wheat grass (*Agropyron*) can be seeded or bought in cubes in pet stores and produce markets. The thick, lush sprouts stand straight and tall and are well displayed in square metallic containers that emphasize their linear look.

Set tray in a warm spot, such as on top of the refrigerator. Check for sprouts after two days and move tray to a sunny spot as soon as they appear. Mist heavily for another week. Wait to water gently until grass is strong enough to resist a light flow.

Turn tray every day for straight growth. When grass is 4 inches tall, tilt tray at an angle and cut off one third of the length with sharp scissors. Nudge clippings away and out of the tray as you cut.

Twice weekly "mowings" encourage dense growth, but only when one third or less of the blade length is removed. More drastic cutting shocks and inhibits growth.

After six weeks or more, begin to shorten blade length little by little if you prefer a shorter stand of grass. Transplant sections of turf into more attractive containers as soon as it achieves a pleasing density.

spring bulbs

Of all the ways that spring renews the garden, the visual impact of fresh color has the strongest effect. One of the most satisfying ways to enjoy explosive hues indoors is through the bright, dancing heads of flowering bulbs. Their unabashed cheerfulness inspires good humor and foreshadows a litany of flowering plants in the days and months to come.

Pert and perky daffodils are never timeworn – they're always welcome in a spring garden. Fill a room with the feel of spring by displaying them with abandon on low tabletops; set them higher on windowsills to add punch to rain-washed vistas.

Plant a creeping thyme, such as *Thymus praecox*, to cover the soil. Be sure to turn the container daily to prevent blossoms from facing in only one direction. Bulb fanciers will want to explore the many cultivars of a species and choose several for a staggered bloom period. Don't overlook miniatures in favor of standard varieties; the latter often grow too tall for indoor use and have weak stems that must be tied.

If you haven't the time or energy to order bulbs in fall and force them for spring, don't let that stop you from planting a bulb garden. Nurseries take care of the job for you. Flower markets, florist shops, and supermarkets carry good selections.

Unless you have outdoor garden space where you can transplant the bulbs after they bloom, discard them. They need long periods outdoors with moisture and fertility to prepare for another round of flowering. Lacking that, future bloom is sacrificed and only foliage appears.

- Bright light
- Slightly moist soil
- Cool temperature
- Discard after bloom

forcing bulbs

Forcing bulbs for early bloom can be as easy as reaching for a glass of water—that is, if paperwhite narcissus, hyacinth, and crocus are your bulbs of choice. Balance any of them on the rim of a glass or narrow vase with just the roots in water, and blooms will force their way to the top as roots trail below. Or set them on a base of pebbles and maintain a water level just below the surface for a larger garden in a dish. Other bulbs need soil and most require a period of winter chill. Anemone, glory-of-the-snow (*Chionodoxa*), lily of the valley (*Convallaria majalis*), crocus, snowdrops (*Galanthus*), grape hyacinth (*Muscari*), scilla, and tulips are others you can try.

For brilliant color and intoxicating fragrance, plant freesias (right). Their sweet aroma regales as each trumpet flower unfurls one by one on an angled, slender stalk arching above narrow foliage. A half dozen or more blossoms on a single stem last for weeks in a cool setting. You can find a freesia variety in nearly any color of the rainbow.

Freesia is notorious for its tall, rather weak flower stems that nearly always call for a supporting stake and a raffia tie when the bulbs are forced indoors. You'll avoid this minor annoyance if you purchase nursery-grown plants, which are always stouter. Here, they are set in aquarium gravel with their roots in water. Fluttering over a topping of pale turquoise beach glass, they appear to float in an ethereal setting of vibrant and subdued tones that speak warmly of spring.

◄ Lily of the valley

Intoxicating scents and nodding, waxy blossoms are irresistible to the springtime gardener. In fall, order roots of lily of the valley (*Convallaria majalis*) for forcing and keep moist and cool until late winter. Pot them up about a month before spring bloom and move them to a warm spot in morning sun.

► Freesia

Freesias begin blooming at the bottom of an angled flower spike. Pinching off each flower as it fades enhances the appearance of new blossoms as they unfurl.

bulb garden plants

▶ Windflower

Bright scarlet petals are the most common, but some varieties of windflower (*Anemone x fulgens*) come in shades of pink and rusty coral. Tubers prefer moist, cool conditions (55 to 70°F) from the time they are planted until they bloom three months later.

▲ Grape hyacinth

Looking very much like a garden of succulent grass, grape hyacinth (*Muscari*) foliage makes way for short spikes of urn-shaped lilac to deep blue flowers that are sometimes fragrant. 'Blue Spike' is compact with double blue flowers; 'Cantab' is lower growing and later blooming.

◀ Daffodil

Tone down the hot sulfur yellows of this old favorite by selecting daffodil (*Narcissus*) cultivars in cooler white, cream, or pale yellows. Turn up the heat with bright orange trumpets. Choose miniatures for undersized arrangements in tiny containers.

daisies by the dozen

Summer heat can be hard on indoor plants — soil dries quickly and leaves turn brown. But you needn't give up your dream of a flowering summer garden. Make it a reality by focusing on easy-care plants. Fortunately, there are resilient species bred to withstand tough conditions and keep the garden going on a tabletop.

Massed together, daisies from a florist create a feeling of abundance and transport summer's sunshine indoors. Shop for them in nursery pots as you would for an outdoor cottage garden.

Chrysanthemums of many species are one of the most reliable daisy-type flowers. Be on the lookout for dwarf varieties in sparkling white with flat or ruffled petals and sprightly yellow centers.

Look for other brightly hued, long-blooming annuals and perennials that coordinate with your color scheme, or stick with versatile neutral tones. One of the best choices is blue marguerite (*Felicia amelloides*), which blooms almost continuously as long as dead flowers are picked off. In a pot, it rarely grows more than 12 inches tall but is likely to spread a little wider by summer's end.

Swan River daisy (*Brachycome*) is another lavender-blue or white delight that agrees to come indoors. Its finely foliaged mounds stay under 1 foot and are covered with summer blooms.

Be prepared to move your daisy garden as summer progresses. The angle of the sun drops as the weeks wear on, and rays should never be blocked or blooms will falter.

- Direct sun or very bright light
- Slightly moist soil
- Average room temperature
- Discard after bloom

colors of autumn

In a fury of color, autumn days forewarn of a time when many outdoor gardeners must leave trowel and spade behind. During the retreat indoors, it's natural to gather together fading stems and branches to eke out a connection with the garden, arranging them inside to finish out the final weeks of fall.

There's another path to follow, one that sustains a growing garden and brings it indoors to last far longer, and that is to fashion a living garden from autumn hues. The rich colors of kalanchoe (far left), rex begonia (center), and croton (*Codiaeum variegatum* var. *pictum*, top right) are echoed in the hues of their earth-toned pots and paint vivid scenes inside the window.

To their year-round color, add pots of specialty, late-season fruiting plants. Some of the most delightful must grow outdoors until fruits set, then they can be brought indoors for autumn decor. A 1- or 2-foot-tall dwarf pomegranate (*Punica granatum*) turns brilliant yellow just as small fruits – more decorative than flavorful – redden. Its vivacity is matched only by that of an ornamental pepper (*Capsicum annuum*) virtually covered with miniature red and yellow hot fruits, daringly edible and packed with potency.

Because the pepper is an annual, discard it after fruits and foliage fade. Pomegranate is a deciduous shrub that enters dormancy with leaf fall. Return it outdoors, prune out the oldest stems in late winter, and wait another year for the promise brought on by spring bloom.

- Bright, indirect light
- Slightly moist soil
- High humidity
- Average room temperature
- Varied life spans

winter cheer

Winter holidays signal a search for special projects and decorations. When that encompasses an arm of the garden, the result is sure to please. Such is the case in the construction of a nontraditional living wreath that has the potential to continue on through warmer seasons or, alternatively, lasts for just a month or two.

Crafting a wreath takes little time or preparation and is similar to planting a moss-filled basket with flowering plants. In this case, lime thyme and succulents join traditional red berries and candles to celebrate the season.

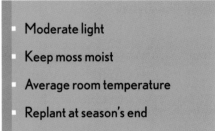

- Moderate light
- Keep moss moist
- Average room temperature
- Replant at season's end

There are no strict rules to follow in selecting plants, but your finished project should prominently feature one striking specimen, another one or two plants with smaller foliage for filling in, and yet another to provide accent color.

Depending on your decorative intent, add late-season fresh or dried flowers or fruits, pinecones or clippings, and any other ornamentation you choose. Make your wreath as elegant or as playful as you wish. To balance the horizontal orientation of the wreath, set tall candles either in the center or within the foliage. You may want to include fittings inside the frame to hold candles upright as you construct the wreath.

WHAT YOU'LL NEED

2-inch pots of succulents

2-inch pots of thyme or other evergreen filler plant

Stems with berries

Plastic sheeting

Sphagnum moss

Dishpan or bowl of water

Wire wreath base

Florist's wire

Dried foliage, flowers, or cones (optional)

Scissors

Waterproof tray

ONGOING CARE

Immerse in water weekly until air bubbles stop floating to the surface, then drain thoroughly. Reposition loose plants, wiring them firmly against the moss. At season's end, replant succulents and filler plants in soil and set them in bright light to recoup until spring, then use them in another garden project.

Before beginning, cover your work area with plastic sheeting and soak moss for at least 1 hour. Gather together plants ahead of time and set them out to try various placements in the wreath. Look for coordinating colors, contrasting texture, and enough foliage to fully cover the form.

Moisten clumps or sheets of moss in a dishpan of water, then position them under wire base and along both inner and outer perimeters, reserving space within the form to hold plants. Wrap wire loosely around the wreath, adjusting moss so it is thick enough at the bottom and sides to prevent soil from spilling through.

Position clumps of succulents in five or six places around the wreath to serve as focal points. Wedge rootballs snugly inside the wire base, firming them with additional moss, as needed, and taking care that rootball does not penetrate moss.

Insert small-leafed filler plants between succulents, leaving space for any accessory plant material that you want to add.

Cover any open area with additional moss, then wrap the entire wreath again, running wire over each rootball under foliage. Trim with scissors as needed.

Immerse finished wreath in water, lift, and drain thoroughly. Display on a waterproof tray.

Winter Wraps

Moss wrapped with florist's wire stays neatly in place and secures plants that nestle inside the frame. Wreaths larger than 12 inches become quite heavy and require more plants.

◄ **Thyme**

Closely set, tiny leaves of lime thyme (*Thymus citriodorous* 'Lime') are perfect for spilling over a moss-wrapped wreath. Thyme doesn't mind drying out a bit between waterings, but it should never be allowed to dry out completely. A finger in the rootball will tell you when it wants refreshing.

► **Bearberry cotoneaster**

Berries of evergreen bearberry cotoneaster (*Cotoneaster dammeri*) borne on long stems are secured inside a winter wreath for bright red accents. Alternatively, use stems from bearberry (*Arctostaphylos uva-ursi*). Clip stems from plants in the ground or from purchased nursery plants. Bright green foliage provides an additional color accent.

▼ **Hens-and-chicks**

Succulents, such as this hens-and-chicks (*Sempervivum arachnoideum* 'Cobweb'), make striking focal points in wreaths. Cluster several 2-inch-wide rosettes at each point of placement. Note that sempervivums are long-lived and grow willingly in an indoor succulent garden.

winter wreath plants

perfect plants, perfect garden

Timely care is one of the keys to success in any garden. Plants can't speak up when they need water or are drowning in excess. Nor can they beg for attention when they're feeling other stress or neglect. But these problems won't arise if you make quick and regular inspections of foliage and soil. Once that becomes routine, you'll detect problems before they get out of control and be ready to act when special care is needed. With your contained garden in full view and within easy reach, care-taking can become a pleasurable pastime.

tending the indoor garden

Artistry in the indoor garden determines how pleased you are with the plants you tend and where you place them in your home, but as with any garden, it takes regimented maintenance to ensure complete success. Careful observation and a willingness to put some assumptions aside go hand in hand with watering, fertilizing, adjusting light, and monitoring humidity.

WATERING – GETTING IT RIGHT

Because more plants die indoors from too much water than from too little, a guiding principle in caring for your garden is this: When in doubt about watering, wait – unless the soil feels nearly bone dry. The safest approach is always to feel the soil first. If it's dry 1 inch or more beneath the surface, it's time to water. Those species that hail from moist tropical or boggy environments are the exception, of course, as they depend on consistently damp conditions for proper growth.

Several factors influence the frequency of watering needs. Non-porous containers and those lacking drainage holes retain water; porous containers and those allowing free drainage lose moisture more rapidly. Summer temperatures prompt plants to absorb water faster and promote evaporation from the potting mix.

But water loss can be just as severe in winter, when heating systems dry indoor air and humidity falls. Households that turn down the thermostat do their plants a favor, unless room temperature drops below 55°F and tropicals respond unfavorably.

Water temperature also affects a plant's growth. Tepid water is best; cold water splashed onto foliage may cause unsightly splotches. Cold water on roots can stress plants enough to slow growth, prevent water intake, and cause root rot.

Although we drink water straight from the tap, the chemicals we can tolerate aren't necessarily good for

Foliage Inspections

Meeting water needs involves a willingness to observe each plant individually, because each species has its own requirements for moisture. It's best to put aside the notion of weekly watering and instead substitute weekly – or more frequent – foliage inspections. Robust color and firm texture indicate that you're on the right track. Brown tips are a common indicator of drought, though they can also result from overfertilization. Overwatered foliage turns yellow. When a plant is overwatered, the roots simply drown in the absence of air and begin to rot, leaving foliage without nourishment and the entire plant facing ruin.

when you're away

Plants never take time off, even if the gardener does. Without a reliable (and experienced) plant sitter, it's still possible to leave an indoor garden behind for up to two weeks if you take one or more of the following precautions.

cotton cording wick

Simple wicking system

- Lower the thermostat to 50°F.
- Move all plants out of direct sun or very bright light but not into darkened rooms.
- Enclose individual pots in a sealable plastic bag with chopsticks holding the bag off foliage.
- Water plants well and move them to a bright bathroom. Fill the tub with several inches of water to supply plenty of humidity.
- Transfer plants to a self-watering pot.
- Set pots on a capillary mat with one end resting in a sink or tub full of water and the remainder stretched out over a water-resistant surface.
- Wick water down into pots from a bottle of water set slightly above plants. Position a long, thin wick, such as cotton cording, from the water to the potting mix (see illustration at left).
- Set clay pots in a larger container filled with wet sphagnum moss. Push the moss through the drainage hole to wick up water from a lower source.

---

plants. Chlorine and fluoride in municipal water supplies have potentially damaging effects. Fortunately for plants, getting rid of those chemicals is a simple matter. They evaporate readily after being exposed to air for 24 hours. This means, of course, that you must have a usable supply on hand in a bucket or bottle ready for your garden when it's thirsty.

Home water softened by ion exchangers isn't as easily altered. It contains salt compounds that won't dissipate and can't be tolerated for the harm they do to plants. Reverse osmosis treatments, by contrast, produce water that is quite safe.

In some parts of the country, well water is often hard and too alkaline for plants, leaving them unable to absorb nutrients in amounts needed for healthy growth.

The ideal water is what plants receive naturally – rainwater. Not everyone is willing or able to collect it on a regular basis, so it isn't universally practical. It's much more convenient to rely on the purity of distilled bottled water.

MOIST, CLEAN AIR

Just as plants depend on moisture in the root zone, so too do they need it around their foliage. Dry air forces plants to lose water rapidly through leaf pores, stressing their system beyond normal limits unless they are dryland natives. To lessen the stress, set containers on a pebble-lined humidity tray partially filled with water, making sure the water level never reaches the pots. Alternatively, run a room humidifier when the heat is high and the air is dry.

Clean air is nearly as important to plants as high humidity. Plants subjected to dust, smoke, kitchen vapors, or chemical fumes may show leaf damage. Many types of air filters remove such bothersome pollutants.

providing nutrients

Plants grow best when given mild doses of water-soluble fertilizer every week or two, but solid, slow-release forms work nearly as well and eliminate measuring and scheduling. Push large pellets to the bottom of a pot with a chopstick (A). Work slow-release granules into the soil with a fork (B). Insert pencil-thin sticks along the side of a container (C). Spray dilute doses of water-soluble fertilizers onto bromeliad foliage (D), but for orchids, use a long-spouted watering can to pour it under the foliage and over the potting mix (E).

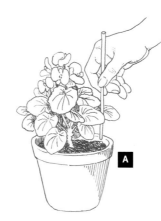

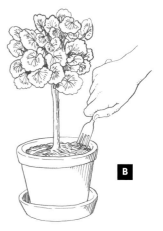

FERTILIZER SUPPLEMENTS

Unlike outdoor gardens, where plant roots reach across a wide area, contained gardens depend on nutrients close at hand. Soilless potting mixes are naturally low in fertility, so you need to add supplements at regular intervals to sustain plant vigor. When nutrients build up or are too concentrated from the start, roots and foliage tips burn and set back the garden, sometimes with devastating effects. A safe approach is to apply an all-purpose fertilizer in very low doses, one half or one quarter of the recommended amount. Specially formulated products, such as African violet fertilizer, are usually mild enough to use as directed on the package. Many gardeners prefer to fertilize with each watering, calculating safe, fractional amounts for each application.

TRACKING LIGHT

Plants depend on a specific light intensity for their very lives. Light, after all, in the process of photosynthesis, is the catalyst for food production, without which plants can't survive. Locating your indoor garden in the right kind of light is one of the keys to its vigor.

Most plants that thrive indoors require bright, indirect light, often filtered through an outside obstruction or an indoor shade. In lower or stronger intensities, foliage is damaged and growth slows. Outdoor plants that depend on direct sun have the same needs when they're brought indoors if they're to perform up to the same level. A dwarf citrus, for example, will fail to bloom and fruit indoors if sun exposure is inadequate. Although sun-loving plants are able to withstand lower light levels for up to several weeks at a time, they must be returned to sunshine if they're to survive.

An east-facing window is an ideal spot for most plants. If morning sun is filtered, plants there enjoy long hours of bright light. A south- or southeast-facing window better serves sun-loving species. Direct sun in a south- or southwest-facing window may be too strong. North-facing windows are suitable only for species that thrive in deep shade.

artificial light

Full-spectrum fluorescent tubes are good substitutes for natural light. They're most effective on racks where the distance they're held above plants can be easily adjusted. Flowering plants require long exposure of 8 or more hours and close proximity of up to 6 inches. Foliage plants require lower light intensity and respond favorably to a light source that is up to 2 feet away.

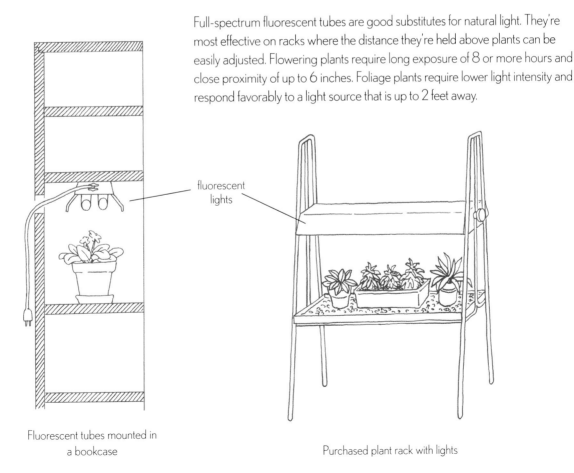

fluorescent lights

Fluorescent tubes mounted in a bookcase

Purchased plant rack with lights

planting and ongoing care

Getting a garden off to a strong start by planting in the right potting mix pays off later when container plants grow to their potential. Indoor gardeners have found that using custom mixes suited to each plant type — orchids and cacti, for instance, have very different needs — gives far better results than relying on just one bag of all-purpose potting soil. When plants respond with active growth, you'll want to maintain their appearance and natural-looking proportions through timely pinching and pruning.

LIGHTWEIGHT SOIL BLENDS

Indoor gardeners are always cautioned against bringing garden soil into the house. The reasons are sound, despite the knowledge that fluffy loam well fortified with compost works wonders in cultivated garden beds outdoors. The main drawback is the mineral matter in soil. When confined inside a container, it compacts and detracts from root health rather than promoting it. Also, the pathogens present in all soils are of no concern in their own ecological niche but when relocated indoors can cause some annoying problems.

Sterilized products purchased in bags are more reliable than garden soil. Of the many types available, soilless blends composed of peat and other lightweight organic and mineral materials are most reliable for indoor plants. They are formulated to provide fast drainage and ample air circulation, but not nutrients.

In certain cases, usually those concerning woody-stemmed plants, a soil-based medium is recommended, especially if the plant will be returning to an outdoor garden after a brief period in the house. Premixed and bagged blends are sterile and are formulated with both organic and mineral matter according to tested ratios. The soil contains a residual amount of nutrients, but regular fertilization is still necessary for plant health and vigor.

Some gardeners prefer to prepare their own potting mix. If you undertake a large-scale project and have room to store extra supplies, that route is more economical. Equal parts of washed sand or perlite, peat moss or fine bark, compost or leaf mold, and minute amounts of dolomitic limestone are typical ingredients in a homemade blend. Pumice or lava rock is frequently added for sharp drainage; vermiculite, for extra moisture retention.

Because soilless products tend to contain very low amounts of fertility, you must provide supplements at regular intervals or your plants will steadily decline. Soil-based mixes contain residual amounts of nutrients beneficial to woody plants and sustain plants to a greater degree.

COMPACTNESS AND CONTROL

Starting out with the right plant is the very best way to keep a garden under control. Before you ever bring a plant home from the nursery, note its growth rate and mature size and settle on a spot where it will grow under optimum conditions. The perfect plant in the perfect place should perform as anticipated.

All plants aren't perfect, of course. Periodic shaping and grooming are nearly always necessary to bring out their best and maintain scale with their surroundings. Pinching off long stems forces buds to sprout farther back on the stem and develop more fullness than plants might normally show. Stems that sprout only from the base must be removed completely to force new growth.

Plants with tall flowering stems, such as orchids, frequently need assistance in supporting the weight of their blossoms. A thin branch or a bamboo cane easily fits in an orchid container; for flowering vines – jasmine and bougainvillea, for instance – use a heavier pole or a metal frame to keep them under control. Tie back plants with either natural-looking raffia or twine and discard plastic ties that come from the nursery.

Cut thick-foliaged clumps from the tops of dracaena, cordyline, and other tropicals as stems lengthen and leaves drop. Treat them as cuttings and return them to the garden after new roots develop.

REFRESHING INTERLUDES

Inveterate gardeners often feel compelled to tend their struggling indoor plants down to the last fallen leaf and bedraggled stem. It's a noble notion, but a sickly garden isn't pretty, and there's a better way to deal with sorry-looking plants: Give them a refreshing change of scene before they're completely desperate or ready for the compost pile.

Plants may appear at their worst in winter, when revitalizing options, such as a heated greenhouse, are limited, but very few improvements occur anyway in plants during their winter rest. They must wait for the mild, restorative weather of spring before changes occur. That's when their genetic programs respond to lengthening days and increasing light levels and a growth cycle begins anew.

encouraging compact growth

Knowing when and how to alter a plant's shape can be puzzling. For example, fast-growing plants, such as herbs, generally need frequent pinching to produce maximum foliage and avert straggly growth. Conversely, too drastic pruning on citrus sacrifices fruit, so restrict routine pruning to wayward twigs only, cutting them off where they meet a main branch.

Pinching stem tips

Pruning uneven growth

Many species benefit tremendously from an outdoor sojourn during their spring growth spurt. After a few weeks – not just a few hours – in bright, filtered outdoor light, they regain their finest glow.

Your own time constraints and the climate where you live, though, may restrict their outings to a few hours each day if you must return them indoors at night. Just make sure that such comings and goings occur during similar conditions to avoid shock. For example, move plants from a warm spot outside to a warm room inside or from a cool patio to a cool porch.

Spring may be ideal for a move outdoors, but mild summer and early-autumn days are also beneficial. A gentle rain or fine-spray washing during any of those times is a bonus.

TEMPORARY REPRIEVE

If you aren't able to arrange the luxury of a plant outing, look for an indoor spot with improved conditions to serve as a refreshing zone during the growing season. An enclosed porch, a bright sunroom, or a window-front table would work.

Pay close attention to sun patterns when you move plants to avoid leaf burn and fast-drying soil. Facing a dearth of alternate sites, consider using artificial fluorescent light, a good substitute for gentle sunshine (see page 143).

There is another approach to rejuvenating an indoor garden; it flies in the face of solid determination to revive faltering plant life, however. Simply toss out plants that have fallen from grace. This isn't a defeat, for gardening isn't a contest. And it isn't terribly frivolous, either, because many plants are short-lived. If it makes you feel better to put them in the compost for another go-around, so much the better.

REVERSING THE SEASONS

Gardeners with favorite outdoor plants that need overwintering sometimes relegate them, leggy stems and all, to the basement and

training plants on wire forms

Timely care yields healthy gardens, but shapely plants depend on a deft hand that coaxes unruly stems and makes judicious snips with scissors and shears. You may need to trim side shoots and tuck in or tie new growth several times a week as you shape standards and topiaries on wire forms.

trust that life will still flow in spring. By planning ahead, you can convert tender plants into attractive specimens for indoor winter gardens – not only plants in containers, but also some that grow in the ground, such as fuchsia, browallia, geranium (*Pelargonium*), and phormium.

Before dormancy sets in or the first frost hits, do any needed pruning, wait a couple of weeks, then dig your plants out of moist ground. Shake off excess soil, prune away long roots, and pot up the plants. In very slow steps, move them inside over a period of one to two weeks. During the last few days, leave them out for only a couple of hours during the day.

Once indoors, isolate the plants and examine them closely for insects, insect eggs, and signs of disease. It's helpful to wash off foliage with a horticultural soap solution to avoid introducing problems into the house.

Another approach is to take cuttings in summer, have them rooted and potted up by fall, and get them ready to grow indoors in winter. In that case, your plants will be much smaller, but you may not have space for large pots anyway. Some genera, such as phormium, are perfectly willing to spend the winter in a vase of water. After several good rinsings, a dousing in a *very* mild bleach solution – just a few drops in a cup of water – and another rinsing, let a few stems join your indoor water garden.

Pets and Plants

A layer of flat river stones or gravel mulch on the surface of the soil discourages house cats from disturbing your plants, especially those in large pots. If you prefer a softer look, try planting a creeping or mat-forming plant with very small foliage, such as miniature English ivy or baby's tears. Covering potting mix with gravel, plants, or sand also discourages relatively harmless but bothersome fungus gnats.

renewing the garden

Some plants manage to adapt easily to an indoor environment and thrive for years and years with little effort on your part. Yet even with the most steadfast care, many plants eventually languish and must be replaced. Others are intended for only short-season displays. Like a bouquet of freshly cut flowers, they bring ephemeral pleasure, are here and gone.

repotting

In time, potting elements break down and roots become crowded. To determine whether a plant needs repotting, invert the container, tap the rim against a hard surface, and turn out the plant. Roots growing out of the drainage hole, bulging up at the rim, or wrapped around the rootball are sure signs that repotting is in order. Fast-growing plants call for inspection every year; slower-growing species, every two or three years.

It's up to you whether you want to move a plant into a larger pot; doing so allows for greater height and width. If you don't, simply turn out the plant, trim the roots, and refresh the soil. Restricting pot size has a dwarfing effect. If you do increase pot proportions, it should never be by more than 2 inches wider or deeper than the old pot.

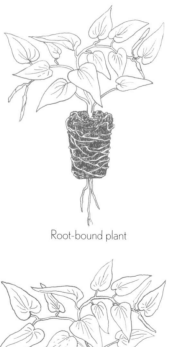

Root-bound plant

Repotted plant

PLANNING FOR A GARDEN'S LIFE SPAN

Short-lived gardens are intended from the start to be fleeting. Some, such as forced bulbs, involve a long preliminary gardening phase that culminates in a burst of color and then is over.

Don't hesitate to treat other indoor plants as short-term garden amusements. Many are as disposable as floral bouquets, less expensive, and easy to pick up as you're shopping for groceries. Those are plants that you will never tire of and will look forward to growing again.

For moderate-term gardens, one or two years is all you should expect from a number of plants, particularly those that normally grow outdoors in temperate climates. Such plants adapt less readily than most tropicals to indoor conditions. Many require a period of winter dormancy and long hours of sunshine in order to prosper. Creeping ground covers, some water plants, most herbs, and flowering perennials will do fairly well with normal bright interior light.

Long-lived gardens are often composed of adaptable tropical species, which constitute the bulk of hardy houseplants. Most thrive in nature in semishaded conditions, which translates to filtered, indirect light indoors. Rain-forest tropicals that depend on elevated levels of humidity may come to mind first, but desert-climate plants may be even easier to grow and longer-lived.

Succulents and cacti of all types, many water plants, ferns, mosses, dwarf mondo grass, African violets, begonias, ivies, orchids, and some bromeliads all live for many years in indoor gardens, as do dwarf citrus and some shrubs and vines that are given long periods of direct sun.

Once you understand the life expectancy of your plants, you can make plans for their future. Specimens in a water garden that you want for a special-effect centerpiece may be able to continue on and on in an aquarium holding tank. Or you may have an outside pond as a constant source from which to replace flagging indoor plants (with the exception of the invasive water hyacinth, which should never be grown outdoors if there is any threat of escape).

Long-lived plants, including desert cacti, may outgrow their welcome if you allow them free rein. In such cases, you may need to discard them if their needles start to encroach on living space, then start again with a younger plant, holding it back the next time in a smaller pot.

ENCOURAGING NEW GROWTH

A garden need not be filled with completely different plants or a change of containers for a renewed look. Judicious trimming of stem tips encourages branching and fresh new growth. If you're looking for increased height — or length, in the case of ivy — trim off side branches only. A constant supply of herbs depends on encouraging fresh new growth. Cut chives all the way to soil level to force new grassy shoots. Cut back lavender halfway to force a second round of flowering.

In general, prune plants during periods of active growth. That means early spring through summer for most species. Watch for buds to swell in late winter on deciduous or semi-deciduous plants, including fuchsia, pink jasmine, hibiscus, and bougainvillea, all of whose long, wispy branches should be cut back severely. Before bud break, do some pruning so that new growth will be more compact. Continue to prune after the first bloom to promote branching and more flowering.

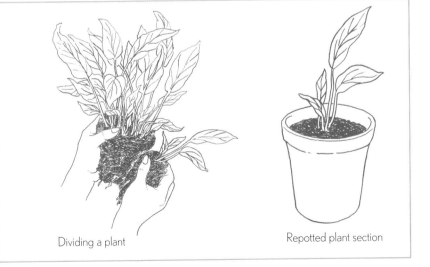

Prolific Growers

Fast-growing species, such as rex begonia, ferns, and plants growing under glass, may develop too rapidly for your garden and be suitable only in their youth. If a plant can be divided, keep the smallest part and repot it, then share the rest with friends.

Dividing a plant

Repotted plant section

propagating

Starting over with small, new shoots and rooted cuttings may sound like taking a slow boat when you'd rather jet off to a full-grown garden. Patient gardeners who have taken this route would disagree, pointing to the fascination they've found in propagating plants. One convincing argument is that you're able to observe the birth of a plant not from a seed but from a lowly leaf or meager tip of a stem. Another is that by dividing an overgrown specimen, you're able to renew its lease on life and produce another plant at the same time. Following such a regimen, you can keep a plant, or at least its clones, going forever.

Leaf Cuttings

Suspend a mature African violet leaf through a plastic cover over a small jar of water. The leaf stalk should be half submerged. Alternatively, set a shorter stemmed leaf into potting mix so that ½ inch of the leaf base is covered. Keep moist until a new tuft of leaves appears, then repot.

Stem Cuttings

Thyme is not long-lived indoors, but you can maintain a constant supply of plants by rooting cuttings at intervals. Strip foliage from the bottom half of a 3-inch stem section and place it in moist sand or perlite. A gentle tug on the stem after three weeks will tell you whether roots have formed.

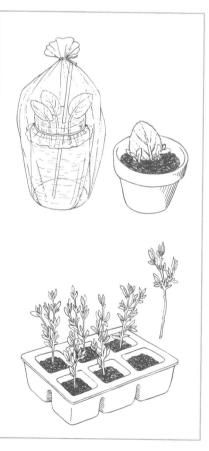

TAKING CUTTINGS

Plants that grow from a single point at the base are most often propagated by stem cuttings taken in spring or early summer. Many plants respond with new growth within weeks after a stem is placed in moist potting soil or a rooting medium of sand or perlite, while others must be treated with a rooting hormone.

Enclose the cutting in a plastic bag for one to three months to preserve moisture and humidity. Open the bag each week to let in fresh air; open it fully as soon as growth begins. Cuttings from roses, geraniums, and jade plant, for example, root faster when they are left in the open air for a day or two to form a callus over the cut stem, then set in a rooting medium.

Stem cuttings should be long enough to include three nodes, or swollen joints where leaves are attached and where new roots form. The upper leaves should remain attached, but completely remove those from nodes placed below soil level. If the attached leaves are large, cut them in half to prevent debilitating water loss.

Leaf cuttings can be made from plants with thick, fleshy leaves, such as African violet and rex begonia. They take longer than stem cuttings (anywhere from two to six months) to produce new plants. Place them in a mini greenhouse or an enclosed plastic bag where fresh air is renewed weekly and humidity is high.

SEPARATING AND DIVIDING

A good many plants, such as cacti, bromeliads, and succulents, do the propagating for you by producing rooted offspring that would develop into colonies were they growing in their native habitats. Propagating them is a simple matter of separating or breaking away the rootlets from the parent plant and repotting the offspring.

Plants that slowly spread by broadening basal clumps must be divided, or cut up into rooted sections and replanted. Only mature plants can be propagated this way, because each section must contain ample foliage and enough stored energy in the root mass to survive on its own.

Plants that develop rhizomes, which are actually underground stems, may also be divided. Each

separating and dividing

When offsets form on bromeliads, cacti, and other succulents, gently pry rootlets loose and pot up offspring as new plants. Divide spreading plants like Scotch moss by breaking or cutting clumps into sections. Cut cleanly through thick rhizomes on plants like rex begonias.

Rooted offspring

Basal clumps

Rhizomes

divided segment should show well-developed rootlets, though some rhizomes are able to sprout new roots where none is growing after they're placed in a potting mix.

Newly separated and divided plants appreciate a little extra attention until they become established in a new pot. Partially enclose them under glass or plastic to raise the humidity level and allow some air circulation. Keep the soil moist — not soggy — and place them in moderate light for two to four weeks.

problem solving

No matter how diligent you are in caring for your plants, problems may still appear. Make regular inspections to catch them at the onset and reduce stress on plants. Most problems originate from improper cultural care, nearly always from overwatering or faulty exposure to light. Changes in leaf color or texture are the first signs of distress. Plants have only a limited number of reactions for several maladies, so always test the soil for moisture as a first step in determining the cause. While leaf drop often signals stress, it's also a natural process. Plants do eventually replace their foliage.

solving cultural problems

IMPROPER CARE	RESULT
Overwatering	Dropped leaves; yellowing leaves; yellow or tan splotches on foliage; wilted foliage; fungus gnats on soil surface; shriveled buds
Underwatering	Drooping leaves; dropped leaves; curled, browned, or brittle leaves; shriveled buds
Too much light	Drooping foliage; yellow or tan blotchy scars on leaves; dropped leaves and buds
Too little light	Pale foliage; undersized new leaves; stems bent toward light; dropped buds
Too much fertilizer	Dropped leaves; browned leaf tips or leaf margins
Too little fertilizer	Undersized new leaves; yellow leaves; dropped buds
Low humidity	Shriveled leaves; dropped leaves; dropped buds; curled, browned, or brittle leaves
Temperature fluctuations	Failure to bloom; brown or black leaf blotches; dropped leaves; dropped buds
Cold water	Brown speckles or blotches on foliage; slow growth
Poor air circulation	Gray mold; dropped leaves

Insect Problems

You can treat insect problems by immersing foliage in soapy water, then rinsing well. To do this, first enclose the pot in a plastic bag, tie it shut over the rim, then invert the pot as you support it, so that the rootball doesn't fall forward. Repeat the process and continue weekly until insects and eggs disappear. Use this method, also, when plants are in prime health to clean dusty and greasy foliage.

dealing with pests

INSECT	PROBLEM	SOLUTION
Aphids	Soft-bodied insects clustered on growing tips; sticky honeydew secretions; curled leaves	Spray with water or soap solution; immerse foliage in soapy water
Mealybugs	Cottony clusters on stems near base of stems and leaves; sticky honeydew secretions; stunted growth; withered, yellowed leaves	Remove with cotton swab dipped in alcohol; spray with water, soap solution, or light horticultural oil; immerse foliage in soapy water
Scale	Crusty bumps on leaves and stems; sticky honeydew secretions	Wash infected areas with soapy water; remove with cotton swab dipped in alcohol; spray with light horticultural oil
Spider mites	Dustlike specks, mostly on leaf undersides; pale stippling on leaves; fine webbing	Wash with miticidal soap solution; raise humidity; lower room temperature
Thrips	Distorted, puckered leaves; brown edges on flowers; specks visible when shaken on white paper	Spray with soap solution; immerse foliage in soapy water
Whiteflies	Minute white flying insects fluttering through foliage; dropped yellow leaves; sticky honeydew secretions	Spray with soap solution every three days; set yellow sticky cards near foliage
Ants and black sooty mold	Attracted to honeydew secretions	Wash deposits with soap sprays and control causal pests

PESTS AND DISEASES

Diseases caused by improper cultural conditions must be solved by correcting procedural care. That may mean discarding a plant and starting over, especially when root health is at stake. A few spots of gray mold are easily picked off, but you must follow up by reducing water and improving air circulation.

Insect problems are different and must be treated. Always begin with the least toxic means possible and never for any reason apply chemical controls indoors. They have no place in the house. If you must use chemicals, apply them outdoors; let vapors dissipate before returning plants to tabletops. Such methods as handpicking, leaf swabbing, and water or soap sprays often take care of minor infestations of aphids, mealybugs, scale, thrips, and whiteflies. Yellow sticky cards, available in nurseries and garden centers, help control whiteflies.

resources

A growing number of suppliers offer plants and products for small-scale, indoor gardens. Nurseries and garden centers are convenient sources, but for specialty and hard-to-find plants and materials, look for suppliers in magazine ads, in garden catalogs, and on the Internet. Consult design studios and decorator shops in your area for unique accessories.

Anita Engberg Pottery
Tel: (707) 546-2434
aengberg@earthlink.net
Fountains, garden sculpture, and several styles of cactus planters (see photo on pages 24-25)

Brent and Becky's Bulbs
7900 Daffodil Lane
Gloucester, VA 23061
Tel: (877) 661-2852
Fax: (804) 693-9436
www.brentandbeckysbulbs.com
A wide variety of bulbs for all seasons

Cliff Finch's Zoo
P.O. Box 54
Friant, CA 93626
Tel: (559) 822-2315
www.topiaryzoo.com
Geometric and animal topiary forms and hints for training vines

Crate & Barrel
Tel: (800) 967-6696
www.crateandbarrel.com
Home furnishings, vases, and decorator items; retail stores nationwide

Fountain Builder
1841 Country Road 977
Ignacia, CO 81137
Tel: (970) 883-5346
www.fountainbuilder.com
Specialty tabletop fountains, basic components and accessories, and operating tips

Four Winds Growers
3373 Sackett Lane
Winters, CA 95694
Fax: (530) 795-1803
www.fourwindsgrowers.com
Dwarf citrus of all types and how-to-grow guidelines

Glasshouse Works
Church Street, P.O. Box 97
Stewart, OH 45778-0097
Tel: (800) 837-2142
Fax: (740) 662-2142
www.glasshouseworks.com
Traditional and unusual plants for every type of indoor garden, for hobbyists and collectors alike

Hedera Etc.
Manatawny Road, P.O. Box 461
Lionville, PA 19353-0461
Tel: (610) 970-9175
E-mail: hedera@worldnet.att.net
English ivy specialist featuring more than
400 varieties

John Scheepers
23 Tulip Drive, P.O. Box 638
Bantam, CT 06750
Tel: (860) 567-0838
Fax: (860) 567-5323
www.johnscheepers.com
Common and novelty bulbs

K & L Cactus & Succulent Nursery
9500 Brook Ranch Road, East
Ione, CA 95640-9417
Tel and Fax: (209) 274-0360
http://home.inreach.com/klcactus
Wide selection of common and unusual
cacti and succulents

Kartuz Greenhouses
1408 Sunset Drive, P.O. Box 790
Vista, CA 92085-0790
Tel: (760) 941-3613
www.kartuz.com
Distinctive and improved varieties of rare
and exotic indoor plants, including many
for small places and terrariums

Kinsman Company
P.O. Box 428
Pipersville, PA 18947
Tel: (800) 733-4146
www.kinsmangarden.com
Planters and liners, topiary frames, pillars,
obelisks, and other unusual items for con-
tainer gardening

Lilypons Water Gardens
6800 Lilypons Road, P.O. Box 10
Buckeystown, MD 21717
Tel: (800) 999-5459
www.lilypons.com
A longstanding and reliable supplier
of water plants of all types

Logee's Greenhouses
141 North Street
Danielson, CT 06239-1939
Tel: (888) 330-8038
Fax: (888) 774-9932
www.logees.com
Renowned for more than a thousand vari-
eties of tropical and subtropical plants

Mannion's Indoor Fountains
P.O. Box 632864
San Diego, CA 92163
Tel: (800) 828-5967
Fax: (619) 280-7711
www.buildfountains.com
Ready-made fountains, as well as supplies,
accessories, and tips for constructing your
own designs; step-by-step instructions for
a new project each month

Marquard Gardens
863 Butler Avenue
Santa Rosa, CA 95407
Tel: (877) 375-8925
Fax: (707) 544-0518
www.marquardgardens.com
Specialty herbs, espaliers, and topiaries

Noah's Ark Topiary
P.O. Box 10213
Largo, FL 33773
Tel: (727) 393-8830
Fax: (727) 392-5483
www.noahsarktopiary.com
A wide variety of topiary wire frames, frames
stuffed with sphagnum moss, and topiaries
fully planted with creeping fig

Owens Orchids, LLC
18 Orchid Heights Drive, P.O. Box 365
Pisgah Forest, NC 28768-0365
Tel: (828) 877-3313
Fax: (828) 884-5216
www.owensorchidsllc.com
Species, hybrids, miniatures, and specialty
orchids

Prosperity Fountain
Neptune in Aquarius
P.O. Box 2486
New York, NY 10009
Tel: (212) 460-5624
www.prosperityfountain.com
A wide range of ready-made fountains
and components for building your own

Richters Herbs
357 Highway 47
Goodwood, ON
LOC 1A0 Canada
Tel: (905) 640-6677
Fax: (905) 640-6641
www.richters.com
Seeds and plants of hundreds of herbs

Santa Barbara Orchid Estate
1250 Orchid Drive
Santa Barbara, CA 93111
Tel: (805) 967-1284
Fax: (805) 683-3405
www.sborchid.com
Thousands of orchids, including many
miniatures, from all over the world

Smith & Hawken
Tel: (800) 940-1170
www.smith-hawken.com
Tools, plants, supplies, and decor for
indoor and outdoor gardens

The Original Livingwreath® Collection
32149 Aqueduct Road
Bonsall, CA 92003-0289
Tel: (800) 833-3981
Fax: (760) 731-3054
www.livingwreath.com
Living wreaths, wreath kits, and supplies

Van Ness Water Gardens
2460 North Euclid Avenue
Upland, CA 91784
Tel: (800) 205-2425
Fax: (909) 949-7217
www.vnwg.com
Bog and water plants and supplies

index

NOTE: Page numbers in **bold** indicate tables; page numbers in *italic* indicate photographs and illustrations.

other storey titles you will enjoy

The City Gardener's Handbook, by Linda Yang. The definitive guide to gardening in small spaces – whether on a balcony, in a container, or in a small yard – covering planting, designing, and maintenance. 336 pages. Paperback. ISBN 1-58017-449-3.

Deckscaping: Gardening and Landscaping On and Around Your Deck, by Barbara W. Ellis. Learn landscaping and planting techniques to turn a deck into an outdoor room, strengthen its link to the garden, create shade and privacy, and make it comfortable and appealing. 176 pages. Paperback. ISBN 1-58017-408-3. Hardcover. ISBN 1-58017-459-0.

Grasses, by Nancy J. Ondra. A complete introduction to using ornamental grasses in combination with annuals, perennials, shrubs, and other garden plants. Includes 24 plans for grass-featured gardens. 144 pages. Paperback. ISBN 1-58017-423-X.

Making Bits & Pieces Mosaics, by Marlene Hurley Marshall. Create unique accents for home and garden by applying broken glass, pottery, tiles, and even buttons to various surfaces. 96 pages. Paperback. ISBN 1-58017-307-1. Hardcover. ISBN 1-58017-015-3.

The Practical Guide to Container Gardening, by Susan Berry and Steve Bradley. Comprehensive information on what types of containers work best for what plants, step-by-step planting techniques, and care and maintenance. Includes complete guidelines for feeding, watering, pruning, staking, propagation, and dealing with pests and diseases. 160 pages. Paperback. ISBN 1-58017-329-2.

Quick and Easy Container Water Gardens, by Philip Swindells. More than 20 elegant designs for creating both still and moving water gardens for a yard, patio, balcony, or tabletop. Step-by-step photos and instructions explain how to choose, install, and maintain pumps and fountains; incorporate fish; maintain healthy plantings; and care for a water garden year-round. 128 pages. Hardcover. ISBN 1-58017-080-3.

Simple Fountains for Indoors and Outdoors, by Dorcas Adkins. Make 20 creative fountains for home and garden – from a small tabletop fountain to a full-sized waterfall – with these clear instructions for choosing materials, installing pumps, and performing finishing techniques. 160 pages. Hardcover. ISBN 1-58017-190-7.

Stone Style: Decorative Ideas and Projects for the Home, by Linda Lee Purvis. Incorporate the elegance and permanence of stone into your home and life with 35 projects using rocks, stones, and pebbles, including a tabletop Zen garden. 160 pages. Hardcover. ISBN 1-58017-375-6.

These and other Storey books are available wherever books are sold, or directly from Storey Books, 210 MASS MoCA Way, North Adams, MA 01247, or by calling 1-800-441-5700. Or visit our Web site at www.storey.com